UNDER PRESSURE

A. Alvarez was born in London in 1929 and educated at Oundle School and Corpus Christi College, Oxford, where he took a first in English.
For a time he researched and taught in Oxford
and America. Out of this came a critical study of
modern poetry, *The Shaping Spirit* (1958; in
U.S.A. *Stewards of Excellence*). Since 1956 he has
lived as a freelance writer in London, travelling a
good deal and making occasional academic forays
to the States – most recently as a Visiting Professor
of English at Brandeis University, 1960. His semi-
nars on Criticism at Princeton University in 1958
resulted in another book, *The School of Donne*
(1961).

Alvarez is now Poetry Editor and critic of the
Observer. He contributed to the *New Statesman*
for ten years and was its Drama Critic from 1958
to 1960. He now writes for the *Spectator*. In 1961
he received the Vachel Lindsay Prize for poetry
from *Poetry* (Chicago) and in the following year
he edited and introduced for Penguins a best-
selling anthology, *The New Poetry*.

A. ALVAREZ

UNDER PRESSURE

THE WRITER IN SOCIETY:
EASTERN EUROPE AND THE U.S.A.

Penguin Books
Baltimore · Maryland

Penguin Books Ltd, Harmondsworth, Middlesex, England
Penguin Books Inc., 3300 Clipper Mill Road, Baltimore 11, Md, U.S.A.
Penguin Books Pty Ltd, Ringwood, Victoria, Australia

—

First published 1965

—

Copyright © A. Alvarez and the contributors, 1965

—

Chapters 2–7 of this book were originally commissioned as features for
the B.B.C. Third Programme. They were broadcast between 1962 and 1964.
Chapter 1 was first published in *Commentary* (March 1965), Chapter 8 in
Encounter (June 1965), and parts of Chapter 6 in *Mademoiselle* (Summer
1964).

—

Made and printed in Great Britain
by Cox & Wyman Ltd,
London, Fakenham and Reading
Set in Monotype Scotch Roman

IN MEMORY OF MY FATHER,

1892–1965

Contents

The public has therefore, among a democratic people, a singular power, which aristocratic nations cannot conceive of; for it does not persuade to certain opinions, but it enforces them, and infuses them into the intellect by a sort of enormous pressure of the minds of all upon the reason of each.

ALEXIS DE TOCQUEVILLE

How can one expect to reason with some generality when the first elements of solid reasoning are not there?

PAUL VALÉRY

Preface

THIS is a book about artists, countries, and the present sense of trouble that pervades them both. I use the word 'artist' loosely. Only a handful of the people to whom I spoke were concerned with the visual arts; most were writers and a fair proportion of these were not 'creative'. That is, critics, philosophers, historians and the rest figure almost as large as the poets and novelists. All of them were intellectuals, in the unabused sense of that term: people to whom ideas are emotionally important. With most I was discussing how these ideas – official, traditional, original, half-perceived – changed and controlled their lives and work. The subject, in short, was the pressures the artists felt themselves to be under and how these altered from country to country.

Perhaps the least high-minded way of describing what follows is as a kind of intellectual travelogue. Apart from the first and last chapters, *Under Pressure* is made up of a series of features broadcast on the B.B.C. Third Programme between 1961 and 1964. This means that it is written in a manner rather different from that of a formal book. Feature programmes have to be spoken, so the style must be looser than usual; they have to be easy to follow, so the issues may sometimes seem a little over-simplified; they also have to be mildly dramatic, since the first requirement of radio is to keep the listeners interested. In cold print all this may well seem tiresome. But there are, I think, at least two good reasons for leaving the programmes alone. First, the radio feature is a valid and often effective way of getting ideas across to a fairly wide public. To recast the programmes in a more conventional form would have meant changing their nature radically and producing another kind of book, another kind of understanding. It would inevitably have taken away some of the liveliness and conflict of opinions which is essential to radio.

Second, since the B.B.C.'s Feature Department has now been disbanded, programmes like *Under Pressure*, which belong neither to Talks nor to Drama, will become, I suppose, increasingly rare. But they are a form of pure radio, with special problems and techniques, special strengths and special weaknesses, quite different from those of television, periodical journalism, or the more long-winded brands of criticism.

When I wrote the first of the *Under Pressure*s I had already done one long feature for the B.B.C. – a portrait – but the problems these programmes posed were new and had to be worked out as I went along. The difficulty was to give a sense of each country and its specialness, and to express personal, often idiosyncratic ideas about it largely through the mouths of other people – without twisting what they said. Those other voices were essential for several reasons: first, it was partly through them that I found out about the countries in question; second, it was on them that I tested my own impressions; third and most important: since even this rather abstract style of radio feature is not a talk, it relies on the variety and balance of different voices to give pace and style to the ideas it is airing. The greater the variety and conflict and inter-cutting, the more effective the thing is as radio. Hence the narration is continually broken by interjections, often very brief, from other speakers. This may be distracting to read but it helps the listener considerably.

The book divides into two distinct halves, not only in theme but in approach. The sections on Eastern Europe are more or less simple introductions to the countries. I had visited none of them before the B.B.C. asked me to; I went knowing very few people, with a tiny handful of introductions and tips, and having only the vaguest – usually inaccurate – notion of what I would encounter. The Writers' Unions were generally very helpful, but I did my best to keep my trips informal and to meet as many different and unofficial people as I could. Some of those I spoke to had international reputations – one was a Nobel Prize winner – more were unknown outside their own countries and some, even at home, had published only in scruffy little magazines. There were poets, novelists, critics, scholars, translators, editors, painters, philosophers, historians, actors, diplomats. There was a genius stage designer in Prague, a logical positivist in Belgrade and a Leavisite in Macedonia. Several had held government posts, even more had been in disgrace, some still were. The conversations were mostly carried on in English or French, sometimes in both, plus a curious, hopeless amalgam of German, Italian, and a handful of vaguely Slavic words I had picked up on the way. The main thing was to communicate, by whatever means. For obvious reasons, only the conversations in English were taped and are used here. Of these, some of the contributors spoke the language with complete fluency, others with great hesitation. I have tampered with the transcripts as little as possible and only cleaned up the grammar where it was absolutely necessary (a listener can get a point from an inflexion which is almost incomprehensible on the printed page).

So far as I could, I kept off politics. My subject was the artist and the pressures exerted on him by the social set-up, history, and traditions of his country. I have no illusions of having analysed any of this in depth. My main intention has been to give an outsider's impression of what the conditions are like for the artist in communist countries, and to do so with as little prejudice as possible. Obviously, for this kind of investigation, dogmas merely get in the way: the bullying edicts and petty tyrannies of communism no more so than the Western brand of dogmatic cold-war-mongering. In disliking both styles of propaganda, I would claim, at least, to be impartial.

The sections on America are different. I have been visiting the States regularly since 1953 and, both privately and as a writer, I have been entangled in many ways with that country. So, however they may look, the broadcasts were written with a great deal of involvement and affection.

There is a second vital difference: I knew almost all the American contributors to the programmes before I went there; many were personal friends of fairly long standing. That and the obvious similarities between life there and in England meant that, most of the time, I was discussing intimately with friends themes and problems common to us all.

I came back from the U.S.A. with more material than I could possibly use, even in three hours of broadcasting. As a result, the programmes tended to become slightly rococo, with any number of arabesques around the central theme. So the things possibly have a more discursive, distracting form than is strictly necessary. But then a single thesis expounded single-mindedly would have been even more false; it would have given no sense at all of the multitudinous contradictions which make the American scene so endlessly stimulating.

The first of the whole series was *Under Pressure: Poland.* This now seems too tentative and out of touch to be worth reprinting, so I have used some of the material from it in the introduction. Elsewhere, I have been careful to date the chapters, since the situation in each country was, and is, obviously fluid. Things now seem much less tense and restive in the communist countries than when I first visited them. Czechoslovakia, in particular, has relaxed out of all recognition. As for the States: I arrived very soon after Kennedy's assassination, when everyone was still obsessed by the tragedy. Now the obsession seems to be with the racial problem. I kept off that, however, for two reasons: first, it was not properly within the scope of my programmes; second, the B.B.C. was at that same time preparing a big series of broadcasts on the Negro in America, and I did not wish to trespass on someone else's preserve.

The theory on which all the programmes are based is outlined very crudely at the start of the last of the American broadcasts, Chapter 7. The first and last chapters of the book are elaborations of this, attempts to deal with some of the themes and implications in more detail than was possible on the radio. Ideally, I suppose, these ideas should be tested on a much wider range of material. But that would have been another book.

I owe a great debt of gratitude to P. H. Newby, Controller of the Third Programme, and Christopher Holme, Assistant Head of Features at the B.B.C. Mr Newby was throughout resolutely sympathetic to improbable suggestions, he encouraged me in the original and very vague idea for the programmes and, despite provocation, scrupulously avoided imposing conditions. Mr Holme produced the things with immense skill and labour, helped me batter them into shape, made countless helpful suggestions and patiently put up both with my illegible scripts and my more impossible demands.

Part I: EASTERN EUROPE

1. Introduction: Poland

YOUR first and last impression of Poland, as of all Eastern Europe, is of a shifting but utterly pervasive sense of trouble. It is as though history had been too much for the place. The continual invasions, divisions, partitions and rape from the east and the west seem to have worn down the national identity and at the same time to have exacerbated it. It is as though the country had survived only by an act of will and the accident of a separate language, almost like a hand-down from the tribal system. Poland, Hungary, Yugoslavia and the rest are all fiercely, clannishly separate and yet constantly absorbed, disappearing into the belly of one vast empire or another: Russian, German, Habsburg, Ottoman. It is no wonder that their precarious, passionate national self-awareness began to reassert itself in its modern form at the height of the Romantic movement.

Nationalism in Poland is a peculiarly literary affair; at times it seems a function or by-product of the Romantic style. It has about it, that is, a continual dramatic urgency, involvement, and excessiveness. During the Nazi occupation, for example, when not only was the cultural life wrenched to a complete halt but the nation itself seemed in danger of being made extinct, the presses of the Underground resistance continued to print, along with the political leaflets and the fighting handbills, poems and short stories, often of considerable subtlety. In the Polish context they seemed as rousing as direct propaganda.

Not that there was anything particularly new in that situation. Literature had been central to the political life of the country at least for the hundred and fifty or so years of the Partition, when the country was split up between Russia, Prussia, and Austria. Then the three forced divisions held together only by the fact that they all used the same language. So literature took on a special function: it became the only public means of preserving the country's identity, its national life, culture and integrity. Henryk Krzeczkowski, a critic and translator, put it this way:

It was a literature with a special aim of educating people, a literature which had to fulfil all the tasks which are normally fulfilled by the State. It was patriotic, pedagogic, moralistic. Its scope was much wider than the scope of literature of normal countries with a normal historical development.

So the Polish writer, whether he wanted it or not, found himself forced into a kind of extreme Leavisite position: the very act of writing made him responsible for the spiritual and political health of his country. But it was a Leavisite position with a difference, as Z. Najder, another literary critic, explains:

Talking about Polish literature and Polish culture in general, one has constantly to repeat that it is almost devoid of the so-called *bourgeois* element. It is traditionally a gentry culture. The origins of this phenomena are very, very complex, but most important is that the Polish intelligentsia originated mainly in the uprooted gentlemen who were losing their privileges and property and coming to the towns in the second half of the nineteenth century. They were the core of the future Polish intelligentsia. When you talk about culture and cultural values in Poland, these values are always connected with the typical gentry code of behaviour: a code of honour, in which the most important notions are those of duty, of honour, of loyalty to your nation, loyalty to your group. Much less important, sometimes virtually non-existent, are the notions of maintaining an economic standard, of preserving life for the sake of preserving life itself.

If this is a peculiarly difficult cultural idea for an Englishman – or any Westerner – to understand, it is less because the principles are foreign than because they don't usually impinge on literature. In England, the gentry values of the squirearchy were, I suppose, taken over in the nineteenth century by the Public Schools, where they became the basic morality for generations of empire-builders. Now, however admirable this training may or may not have been, it never had much significant influence on serious creative work. But in Poland these values of national duty, responsibility and self-sacrifice were not only behind the fantastic heroism, which became almost a national habit, they were also the basis of some of the best literature. It is as though the finest flower of the Great Tradition were Rudyard Kipling.

Granted this brand of nostalgic conservatism is only one force at work in Polish cultural life. Since the country regained its independence in 1919 literary chauvinism has been offset by equally vigorous irritation, a desire to have done with local issues and take part once again in the larger European cultural explosion. Hence the fetish of nation is, in times of relative political ease, balanced by a fetish of experiment. The Poles pride themselves on being the Eastern outpost of Western Europe, prime defenders of the *avant-garde*, 'the French of the East'. Yet however way-out the fashions, Polish artists have never quite shed the inheritance of a time when, in Najder's words, 'All political discussions happened in novels and poems. There were no parties, but there were writers'.

That is more or less their position now, as it is also the position of writers in Russia and the rest of Eastern Europe. Under any one-party system which is not totally repressive, the arts become the most efficient way of airing protest and exposing abuses which are not officially recognized. Witness, for example, the work of Solzhenitsyn and Yevtushenko, which is often more interesting to the Kremlinologist than to the literary critic. In Poland, of course, the arts are by no means the only safety valve. It is a nation of chronic grumblers. They seem to regard Russian dogmatism and acquiescence as just another proof of the Russian lack of humour, imagination and fire; in contrast, the endless complaining of the Poles is a source of national pride.

But the marriage of the arts and politics in Poland goes beyond any accident of the present political set-up or any Marxist theory of social awareness. It is a habit of mind which neither writers nor audience can shed, however politically indifferent, irresponsible, apathetic, or plain ignorant they feel themselves to be. Just as in the West anyone will give you a quick, psycho-analytic breakdown of anything, so in Poland it is impossible to write even about the birds and the bees without someone reading into it a political metaphor or allusion. Polish art runs instinctively to allegory. It is all, whatever its appearance, written in what they call 'Aesopian language', in which each detail can always be translated into terms of something else – something relevant to the immediate Polish situation. Hence when a scholar like Jan Kott writes about Shakespeare's Histories, in the West it is hailed as a revolution in Shakespearean criticism, while in Poland it is treated as political comment – as though there were an implied erratum: 'For "Tudor" read "Polish" throughout.'

Or consider a film like Roman Polanski's *Knife in the Water*. On this side of the Iron Curtain it was regarded as a masterpiece of hip alienation, the final cool analysis of the failure of any member of the classic Oedipal triangle – successful husband, young wife, younger interloper – to break through his own self-enclosing indifference. With less formal chastity and more invention, Godard might have directed it; with more formality still and no humour at all, Antonioni. But in Poland it was interpreted as a parable of the generations: the husband a successful party man, worldly, accommodating, faintly corrupt, versus the disengaged, cynical, footloose, be-jeaned youth, representative of a political generation which had not been in the war: both competing for the favours of the young wife – the new, post-war Poland? – who swayed poignantly between them.

This perennial Polish game of Hunt-the-Symbol may at times be all very intriguing, but it is equally often irritating and sometimes debilitating. For it means that the arts flourish only in a context of continual double-take: their energies, like their statements, invariably qualified and mostly undercut by a kind of nagging sophistication. No doubt this is a necessary antidote to the provincialism and

narrowness of official communist art; sophistication becomes a token of independence. But it can often be cultivated with an intensity which seems almost naïve.
Avoiding the hack positions of the party, they parody a
Weston chic which is, in the context, equally meaningless.
Their endlessly talkative energy gets frittered away in
deviousness.

But all these intricacies and allegories are valuable for
one thing: they are a kind of Polish Declaration of Independence. Politics may be inescapable – however nominally
escapist the art may seem – but the dogmas are never
taken seriously, for the simple reason that they are never
accepted single-mindedly. Despite their patriotic idealism
and their intense awareness of the political reverberations
of their every word, the Poles remain curiously resistant to
ideology. Outside official circles you find socialism without
Marxism, or Marxism only as a starting point for systems
more idiosyncratic, undogmatic, and usually existential.
When I remarked on this to a philosopher in Warsaw, he
replied, 'Socialism in Poland is a thing, a fact like bread
and stones and houses. You cannot make an ideology,
a philosophy, out of a thing.' So in place of any clear
system of beliefs, the Poles, who are the least easily led of
all Eastern European nations, derive from the prevailing
dogma a certain sense of resistance, a limiting edge
on which to test their personal interpretation of things.

Marxism as theory, allegory as nervous tic, and an over-
developed political self-awareness all guarantee that the
sense of trouble which dominates Polish intellectual life
should define itself steadily in terms of objective, and
usually intrusive, social realities. This is not quite such an
obvious process as it sounds. For the whole movement of
avant-garde Western art during the last half-century has
been one of a steady internal migration. Even our most
politically minded writers seem to recreate society in
terms of their own selves, from the outside in, as though
their environment were a wide-screen projection of their
inner tensions. In Poland, despite its Western bias in

artistic styles and preoccupations, precisely the reverse happens: the artists recreate themselves in terms of the public world; social facts become the equivalent of psychic phenomena, with the same inwardly reverberating power and inescapability. If there is a radical difference between the arts on either side of the Iron Curtain it is less in the kinds of pressure which impel the artists than in the directions in which those pressures force them.

For the casual visitor, the first glimmerings of the Polish sense of trouble come from the mere look of the place: the hopeless, deep-rooted drabness of everything. In many ways, Warsaw is one of the liveliest capitals in Europe: theatres, cinemas, and art galleries teem with dissidence and life; the jazz is excellent, the dancing modish, the young people uninhibited, quarrelsome, bloody-minded; the University seethes with argument, the artists' clubs with gossip. Yet if this talkative city of beautiful girls is spiritually like Paris in the twenties, physically it is like nothing so much as London in 1945. Drabness is all: in the food, the clothes, the discomforts. There are still wastelands of cleared devastation, rebuilding is slow and shoddy, there are few cars on the streets, fighters instead of airliners fly overhead, the shops are poorly stocked, the restaurants awful and life generally hard (this, anyway, was my impression in 1961 and '62).

Part of this shoddiness, no doubt, is due to the strain of converting what had been before the war a more-or-less eighteenth-century society into a modern industrial economy. But a greater part still is a survival of the utter devastation of the Nazi occupation. There is no need to set out here the details of the total brutality of those five years,* the barest recital of the facts will do: one person in

* There is an excellent short history by two Polish Professors of Law, based mostly on evidence produced at the Nuremburg trials, *Nazi Rule in Poland 1939–1945*, by Tadeusz Cyprian and Jerzy Sawicki, Warsaw, 1961. For those with strong stomachs there is also a pictorial record of the occupation and the concentration camps, *We Have Not Forgotten*, Warsaw, 1960.

five – six million out of the thirty million population – was killed; dozens of villages were completely destroyed and their inhabitants massacred, in the style of Lidice and Oradour; Warsaw itself was razed and emptied of its million inhabitants, the Nazis boasting that they would make it into 'a second Carthage'; in 1940 the Governor-General, Hans Frank, initiated 'Operation AB' which aimed at the total elimination of the country's intelligentsia; most of the Nazi concentration and extermination camps were situated in Poland; and so on. Perhaps the clearest distinction between the savagery of the Nazi rule in Poland and that in other occupied countries was made by Frank himself when, in a Press interview in February 1940, he boasted about the difference between his system and that which obtained in the Protectorate of Bohemia and Moravia:

In Prague, for instance [he said], large red posters were put up announcing that seven Czechs had been shot today. Whereupon I said to myself: If I wanted to have a poster put up for every seven Poles who were shot, the forests of Poland would not suffice for producing the paper for such posters. Yes, we had to act harshly.*

So if Poland still seems under the shadow of war twenty years after its end, this is not just because the party has kept the wounds open for its own anti-German ends, nor is it because Poland, being scarcely industrialized before 1939, found the devastation too much for it economically.† The reason lies, instead, in the quality and

---

*Nazi Rule in Poland 1939–1945, p. 100.

†The reverse is true of Germany, as Hannah Arendt has pointed out: 'The so-called "economic miracle" of post-war Germany [is] a miracle only if seen in an outdated frame of reference. The German example shows very clearly that under modern conditions the expropriation of people, the destruction of objects, and the devastation of cities will turn out to be a radical stimulant for a process, not of mere recovery, but of quicker and more efficient accumulation of wealth – if only the country is modern enough to respond in terms of the production process. In Germany, outright destruction took the

universal scope of the outrage. A young poet, Leszek Elektorowicz, casually remarked to me, without a trace of drama or self-pity:

I think almost every family in Poland was touched by these misfortunes. For instance, my father was killed in the concentration camp in Grossrosen, my mother was in Ravensbrück and came back after 1945. And I think my position was the same as every young person in Poland.

What, in short, occurred in Poland between 1939 and 1945 has survived and pervades the country still as a kind of collective trauma. It's as though some psychic change had taken place in the nation itself, a curious deadening in some areas, hardening and avoidance in others. If the return to health after the crack-up has been tentative, painful and far slower than anyone could ever have believed, it has also left a shadowy area of shock, disbelief and alteration.

The truth is that the Nazi crimes were on such a scale and at such a remove from sanity that something rather odd occurred: even the people who directly suffered from them were unable, when it was all over, quite to believe what had happened. Those freed from the concentration camps came, after a while, to disbelieve even their own agony; in the context of relative normality it all began to seem a hallucination. So the Poles have continually to remind themselves of the appalling, almost grotesque, realities.

---

place of the relentless process of depreciation of all worldly things, which is the hallmark of the waste economy in which we now live. The result is almost the same: a booming prosperity which, as postwar Germany illustrates, feeds not on the abundance of material goods or on anything stable and given but on the process of production and consumption itself. Under modern conditions, not destruction but conservation spells ruin because the very durability of conserved objects is the greatest impediment to the turnover process, whose constant gain in speed is the only constancy left wherever it has taken hold.' *The Human Condition*, 1958, pp. 252–3.

Since there are obvious political ends to be served by this, there is even a Department of Martyrology devoted specifically to the job. Auschwitz, for example, has been transformed, with great tact, into a museum. On Sundays excursion buses full of workers, tourists, and their children, file through the blocks and the crematorium, pass the cells and reconstructed dormitories; they peer through plate-glass at mountains of hair, suitcases, boots, artificial limbs, spectacles, babies' clothes, children's toys. They shuffle and stare and whisper and, by assuring themselves that the brute facts do exist, they are taught a violent lesson in politics.

But the facts themselves represent an experience, or a violation of experience, which is beyond artistic expression. Only the short-story writer and poet Tadeusz Borowski managed to cope directly with the concentration camps and yet make artistic sense of them. And his method was that of total moral nihilism. Although he is said to have behaved with considerable heroism in Auschwitz, he seemed able to accept his experience there only by a form of artistic self-destruction. In his stories, he, the narrator, is presented as a bastard among bastards: greedy, ruthless, unprincipled, and defended against the suffering around him by a hard shell of anger and contempt. Borowski's almost toneless recording of the facts manages to imply, by its very blankness and acceptance, a level of horror which a more sensational method could not begin to touch. I have written in another essay that 'around Borowski's stories there is a kind of moral silence, like the pause which follows a scream'.* It is precisely that silence, shock and lingering awareness of what was recently intolerable that concerns the most serious and imaginatively ambitious artists in Poland now.

* 'The Literature of the Holocaust', *Commentary*, November 1964. I was trying to analyse in detail the various ways in which the concentration-camp experience has been coped with in imaginative terms. My theories are slightly beyond the scope of this introduction but very much relevant to it.

Over the last few years in the West, particularly in America, the arts have become more and more concerned with breakdown. Poets like Robert Lowell, Sylvia Plath, and Anne Sexton, painters like the abstract expressionists, are attempting to give coherent artistic form to great reservoirs of feeling – destructive, manic, paranoid – which are shut off from more-or-less normal life and more-or-less traditional art forms, but are released in breakdown, or even in psycho-analysis. The Poles, in contrast, are approaching the same problem from the opposite direction. There the psychic explosion took place within the nation itself. It was a factual breakdown, deliberately induced by another nation, historically documented, politically explainable and, for a large part, ethnically motivated. But the violence and horror of the experience is no less extreme for being objectively *there*, outside. The artists have to come to terms with it, contain it and in some degree regulate their own understanding of ordinary life by it.

So there is, I think, in the best Polish art, the same inwardness and sense of complexity, the same tanglement, unease and probing individuality as you find in the best modern Western art. But with one major difference: it is directed outwards. Zbigniew Herbert, who is, in my opinion, one of the most talented poets in Europe, East or West, summed this up in his poem 'Our Fear':

> Our fear
> does not wear a night shirt
> does not have an owl's eyes
> does not lift a casket lid
> does not extinguish a candle
> does not have a dead man's face either
>
> our fear
> is a scrap of paper
> found in a pocket.
> 'warn Wojcik
> the place on Długa Street is hot'

our fear
does not rise on the wings of the tempest
does not sit on a church tower
is earthy

it has the shape
of a bundle made in haste
with warm clothes
provisions
and arms

our fear
does not have the face of a dead man
the dead are gentle to us
we carry them on our shoulders
sleep under the same blanket
close their eyes
adjust their lips
pick a dry spot
and bury them

not too deep
not too shallow*

The implication of this poem is that madness and dis-integration are all on the outside, in war, society, political intrigue. Human beings themselves are oases of ironic sanity and mutual tenderness. This has been Herbert's theme from the start when, at the age of fifteen, he wrote a very beautiful poem about a couple making love as the bombs fall. And that ultimate existential gesture – as though a kiss could annihilate annihilation – is the clue to all his work: war and the human thing are poised equally and unresolvably. But as he has matured as a writer, that outer frame of social reference has become more insistent, inescapable and accepted:

FORTINBRAS'S ELEGY

Now that we're alone we can talk Prince man to man
though you lie on the stairs and see no more than a dead ant
nothing but black sun with broken rays

* Translation by Czesław Miłosz.

I could never think of your hands without smiling
and now when they lie on the stone like fallen nests
they are defenceless as before The end is exactly this
the hands lie apart The sword lies apart The head apart
and the knight's feet in soft slippers

You will have a soldier's funeral without having been a soldier
the only ritual I know at all
There will be no candles no singing only cannon-fuses and bursts
Crape dragged on the pavement helmets boots artillery horses
drums drums I know nothing exquisite
those will be my manoeuvres before I start to rule
one has to take the city by the neck and shake it a bit

Anyway you had to perish Hamlet you were not for life
you believed in crystal notions not in human clay
Always in spasm asleep you hunted chimeras
wolfishly you crunched the air only to vomit
you knew no human thing you did not know even how to breathe

Now you have peace Hamlet you accomplished what you had to
and you have peace The rest is not silence but belongs to me
you chose the easier part an elegant thrust
But what is heroic death compared with eternal watching
with a cold apple in one's hand on a narrow chair
with a view of the ant-hill and the clock's dial.

Adieu Prince I have tasks a sewer project
and a decree on prostitutes and beggars
I must also elaborate a better system of prisons
since as you justly said Denmark is a prison
I go to my affairs This night was born
a star named Hamlet We shall never meet
what I will leave will not deserve tragedy
It is not for us to greet each other nor bid farewell
                We live on islands
and that water these words what can they do What can they do
   Prince*

    The debate between Fortinbras and Hamlet – between
the man of action and political sense and the romantic
idealist, ineffectual dreamer and tragic hero – is perhaps

* Translation by Czesław Miłosz

the dialectical centre of contemporary Polish art. The more Fortinbras seems to be the necessary spokesman for the situation, the more urgent is his own need of Hamlet, and the more poignant his understanding of their utter separateness.

Herbert's steadily detached, ironic and historically minded style represents, I suppose, a form of classicism. But it is a one-sided classicism, based not on order matching order, a regulated style displaying the regularity of the world, but on a strict and wary attitude to a situation which is at best prone to romanticism and at worst a violation of all sanity. It is a way of coping coolly with facts which could easily slide out of control; it is also a viable personal alternative to the dogmatic or theoretical answers of orthodox communist literature. In a way, Herbert's poetry is typical of the whole Polish attitude to their position within the communist *bloc*; independent, brilliant, ironic, wary, a bit contemptuous, pained.

2. Hungary (1962)

At the request of some of the Hungarian contributors, I must emphasize that in the following chapter – as everywhere else in the book – the interviews were taped separately in private conversations with me. Most were made in Budapest where the writers, officially and unofficially, were most helpful and informative. Unlike the other chapters, however, three interviews were taped in London: those with Paul Ignotus, George Pálóczi-Horváth, and George Gömöri. Obviously, there was an extreme divergence of views between the writers in Budapest and the exiles. Neither group wishes to be associated with or held responsible for the opinions of the other.

A.A.

*

I DON'T quite know what I'd expected of Budapest; something grim and beleaguered and restless, I suppose. Such is the efficiency of our propaganda. I was wrong; or rather, it was grim, it was restless, though at first it didn't seem so. When I arrived the air was thick and black with thunder. There were no buses or taxis at the airport and scarcely any people. I hitched a lift with an English businessman, and his driver lost the way in the inevitable industrial slums. They had that oddly empty, grey poverty peculiar to the People's Democracies. It has something to do, quite simply, with the lack of cars on the streets. It also has something to do with the suddenness of a good deal of the industrialization which has taken place, so that the filth and ugliness seem as gratuitously imposed on the landscape as they must have done in nineteenth-century England. They haven't had time to take root.

So I arrived in Budapest through the back door. And the back door is still scarred and battered from the 1956 troubles. The front door, however, is not. Budapest is a remarkably beautiful city and a remarkably comfortable one. The Danube cuts it in two: huge, fast-flowing, and served by elegant water-buses. On one side are the hills of Buda, dominated by a great cliff with a bad statue and a good restaurant on top. Buda itself is full of villas – whole ones for party and embassy officials, bits of ones for writers and the rest of the official *élite*. There are trees and flowers everywhere. The lilac was in bloom and, by night, the nightingales sang startlingly. This was not the darkness at noon I had expected.

On the Pest side of the city, the business area, the boulevards are wide and crowded, the people well dressed, and the shops full both of consumer goods and of customers determined, apparently, to consume them. On nearly every building are the marks of the '56 fighting: curlicues knocked away, stonework pitted by bullets, grey scars where rifts have been badly patched with cement. But no one notices them any more, no one wants to be reminded. On May Day the parade shuffled past decked with coloured paper flowers and banners saying 'Peace', 'Long live May 1st'. There were no pictures of Khrushchev, no 'Long live Kádár'. The cult of personality is, for the moment, dead. Just banners saying 'Peace' and a rather careless holiday atmosphere of disorganization and drink.

'All I want is to be left alone, to be left in peace,' said one of the writers. After '56, like nearly everyone else, he had been in prison. Now he was out again and living very comfortably – a beautiful flat in Buda, a pretty wife, a maid, flowers blooming in at the window. He was still a Communist, but no longer active in politics. He only wanted to get on with his work. And he was typical of nearly everyone I met. The intellectuals, at least, are much less worried or frightened by the A.V.H. – that is, the secret police – than they are by well-meaning foreign meddlers who might upset that delicate balance of Hungarian good living. For example, I was unfortunate to follow in the tracks of a storm-trooper from one of our cold-war journals who had been in Budapest the previous summer. He had seen and talked freely to everyone. Then he went back and wrote what was, by any standard, a wildly indiscreet account of his visit, implying that all the writers he met – whose names he gave – were champing against the régime, yearning to get out of the Russian winter and under that cosy American umbrella. Perhaps he was being oversubtle; more likely, he was being over-naïve. So far as I can judge, all he had done was translate native Hungarian cynicism into an idealist political language which simply does not exist in the country. He had also done harm. Not that anyone was popped into jail – which they would have been had the implications of his article been true. But people were annoyed, embarrassed, a bit frightened, and many writers had foresworn visiting foreigners altogether; they either politely pleaded illness, or they would talk only on the understanding that what they said was not for publication.

I mention this because it is essential for understanding what, I think, is the mood of present-day Hungary. Certainly, the A.V.H. is still there, though less blatantly than it used to be; certainly, there are still many political prisoners, though fewer than there used to be; certainly, those who are not unshakeably with the régime can't get passports to travel abroad; certainly, as in any occupied country, the Hungarians resent the presence of Russian troops and the pervasiveness of Russian influence in their national life: even more, they resent the brutality of the final Russian quelling of the '56 revolution. But no one in Hungary would want to reverse the other, wider social revolution which has taken place since the end of the war. No one, that is, would want to return to the near-feudalism which obtained before and during Horthy's neo-Nazi régime. Even as devoted an anti-communist as the Hungarian refugee, Paul Ignotus, readily admits this:

IGNOTUS: Even those who feel strongly against the present régime and those who feel less strongly against it, I think, would all agree that nothing of the sort of feudalist, semi-

feudalist capitalism of pre-war Hungary, or even of capitalism as we know it, would be restored and should be
restored. I think there's no gainsaying this. It's simply
the totalitarian character of the communist régime they
dislike. And I would say that those who sparked the 1956
revolution off were against the then existing régime, not
because they found it too socialist but because they didn't
find it genuinely socialist. It was really a revival, in a
way, of the old Hungarian Jacobite or Fabian or liberal–
socialist tradition.

A.A.: This liberal–socialist tradition is linked also with a
tradition of more-or-less failed revolutions: the Kossuth
revolution against the Hapsburgs in 1848; the abortive
attempt to establish a Hungarian soviet in 1919; the tragic
affair in 1956. But this pattern of political idealism and
heroic failure is deceptive, as another Hungarian in London,
the political commentator George Palóczi-Horváth, says:

PALÓCZI-HORVÁTH: We have revolutions which seem
madness to start and which look like utter failure but
which, in historical perspective, prove to be sometimes
more successful than eminently successful revolutions. In
1848–9 we wanted to have an independent Hungary with
or without the Austro-Hungarian monarchy, and the outcome of that revolution was really quite an independent
Hungary. By the beginning of the twentieth century, the
Viennese had already started to complain about Hungarian
imperialism. The same in '56: when on October 23, 1956,
we marched and protested, we never thought that we
could beat the Soviet Union, we never wanted to have an
armed revolt and we never hoped to get out of the Soviet
sphere of influence. We wanted to have an easier, more
colourful, freer life: more travel, more freedom, less party-
bullying; and as you have been there now and you know
by reading what sort of despotism there was before, I
think it pretty well came about – mainly because of the
revolution. When we were marching on that revolutionary

protest march in the afternoon of the 23rd, if anyone would have told us that, in five or six years, life would be in Hungary as it is now, we would have been very pleased because it would have accomplished at least a great deal, if not everything that we wanted to achieve. And again if anyone had told us that by midnight we would be fighting or approving of fighting we would have thought him stark staring mad. We never thought of attacking the Soviet Union and Soviet troops; it just came about.

A.A.: The '56 revolution, in short, was a socialist reaction against the reign of totalitarian police terror under the Stalinist Rakozi. It was a left-wing affair; the freedom fighters were Marxist intellectuals, students, and factory workers. Indeed, a number of the more right-wing elements kept out at first because they felt it was an in-party fight. There is a story that when a Russian soldier asked one of the student freedom fighters what his inspiration was, the boy replied 'Russian films about the Russian revolution'. But in terms of the results achieved, much of the irritation which came to a head in '56 may have had a quite simple and practical cause. As a nation, the Hungarians have two overwhelming flairs: for music and good living: they have produced Bartók and Kodály; they are also great cooks, great eaters, great wine-bibbers. Now, between 1948 and 1956 these latter refinements were denied them. The living conditions were intolerable; there were great shortages everywhere, and those who could afford luxuries were suspect. It is possible that bad cooking was as potent a cause of the '56 uprising as police brutality.

All that has changed. Relatively few of the political demands of the revolution may have been met, but life in Hungary, compared with that in other Eastern European countries, is extraordinarily comfortable. They say that in October 1956 the Hungarians and the Poles changed roles: the Hungarians, that is, acted with the lunatic heroism which is normally a Polish speciality, while the Poles, almost incredibly, played a Hungarian waiting game.

Since then both countries have got revisionism of a kind. In Poland, the revisionism is intellectual and spiritual: they have some of the most original and independent poets, philosophers, and film-makers in the whole of Europe. But life there is still hard: food is poor and there is nothing much in the shops. In Hungary, on the other hand, the party line still more or less goes; such originality as there is is hedged by endless provisos, double-talk and ironies so subtle as to take in themselves. Revisionism came in terms of physical comfort: excellent restaurants, smart clothes, crammed shops. The rest, alarmingly, is cynicism. Yet this, according to Ignotus, is a national characteristic:

IGNOTUS: You see, Hungary has been always a country of heroes and corruptionists. Their nobility, which for a long while was Venetian, had always to make the best of the fight between the Ottoman empire and the Habsburg empire, making pacts with one against the other, playing one against the other and then indulging in very heroic deeds against either of them or both. Now I think that you would in some ways find the same thing in present-day Hungary. There is a cult of the heroic. You would find both heroism and corruption mostly, I think, if you started a little drinking with them. Then in often quite a sloppy way they would start boasting about their heroism – which, though they may do it in a sloppy way, is real, I must add. And at the same time they would indulge in absolutely cynical witticisms for which not only that sort of noble-men's tradition is responsible but also, to the same extent, a factor which was very important in Hungary in intellectual life, the Jewish influence.

A.A.: The Jewish influence is everywhere, in the social habits, in the intense cultural life, above all in the humour. The battle is between Magyar romanticism and Jewish scepticism. When all other battles have been lost there remains the fight to survive comfortably in the teeth of one's enemies. Idealism, in short, is modulated by material considerations or regulated to them. Where there is comfort there isn't usually trouble. Everything else is arrangeable. And this was summed up by Kádár himself with the aphorism: 'Those who are not against us, are for us.'

PALÓCZI-HORVÁTH: People in Hungary or people in the Soviet Union see that they cannot take responsibility for their régimes; and there seems to be an agreement about that. After all, the Berlin Wall shows that the division of Europe is final: no one does anything about it, so people have to do their best to get along with their régime, whether they approve of its politics or not.

A.A.: For the Hungarians there is no longer a question of choosing between one armed camp or another, even if they wanted to. It is simply a matter of living as well as possible with what they have. And this has been a constant element in Hungarian life. After all, the country has had hundreds of years of practice in being occupied. It was overrun by the Turks in the sixteenth century. When the Turks were finally thrown out, the Habsburgs took over. Not until 1919 did Hungary become a fully independent country. Péter Nagy, a literary critic, describes this inheritance:

NAGY: It was a bastard society and a bastard economy too, partly bound by the great estates which put their claws on the whole society and partly bound by the German imperialism which hindered the development of genuine Hungarian capitalism.

A.A.: The result of this social–economic bastardy and constant occupation by foreign powers is a curiously centreless quality of national life. It is as though, in some Kafkaesque way, the country didn't quite exist. Or rather as though it existed only by virtue of the cynicism and cleverness by which the Hungarians have adjusted to adverse conditions. Apart from that, its only other abiding marks of identity are its music, its very eminent intellectuals and the strangeness of an impossibly difficult language, which is related to practically no other European tongue except Finnish. The consequence – according to Iván Boldizsár, writer and editor of the excellent *New Hungarian Quarterly* – is an overpowering sense of isolation:

BOLDIZSÁR: I had the feeling in England that you are trying to lose some of the Great Power complexes you have. And sometimes I have the feeling we shall lose some of our small nation complexes, which is even more difficult. We believe nobody knows anything about us, and I am afraid we are right.

Every Hungarian poet has a suffocating feeling of loneliness: not to be understood, except by his compatriots. And this is a strange feeling you cannot translate, you cannot explain, because we are really a very small nation. You are flirting with the idea of being a small nation. We really are.

A.A.: This feeling of loneliness is accentuated, as I said, by the isolation of the Hungarian language. And that, in itself, was doubly isolated because until the middle of the nineteenth century, the official language was still Latin. Tibor Szobotka, who teaches English literature at the University of Budapest, describes this:

SZOBOTKA: There were two parallel languages in the course of the centuries, Latin and Hungarian. Now, Hungarian was more or less connected with the simple people, the peasants. The language of the parliament and of the upper classes, the landed gentry, the nobility, was the Latin. And that lasted for a pretty long time. It was abolished after 1848, after the Hungarian revolution of Lajos Kossuth.

The language of bureaucracy and legislation was, of course, Latin. Well, I wouldn't dare to say that at home and in the family it was used in the same way as Hungarian, but it gave more pomp and more ceremony and more emphasis.

Latin was an instrument of conservatism and was used by certain reactionary classes and types. The infiltration of modern European thought by means of other Western languages was held up by the use of Latin.

A. A.: This linguistic peculiarity was one of the reasons why Hungarian writers have always been so deeply involved in politics; the use of the language in itself was a political gesture.

SZOBOTKA: The feeling was that they should make themselves also culturally independent from the Habsburg empire, which of course meant at the same time that they wanted to make themselves independent from German literary and ideological influences.

A. A.: George Lukács, Hungary's leading Marxist philosopher and literary critic, suggested to me that Petöfi's 'John the Hero' was doubly important in its day because, for the first time in Hungarian poetry, a peasant hero was using the peasant language; he was also seen in himself as the centre of spiritual and patriotic regeneration. Even Tolstoy, in whose imaginative universe the peasant figured so passionately, filtered his simple strengths and virtues through the sensibility of an upper-class intellectual – through a Pierre or a Levin. Not to do so was a political act. Certainly, in Petöfi's time the political implications were clear enough. He was one of the leaders in the 1848 war of independence and died in battle. The second greatest Hungarian poet of the time, Petöfi's friend János Arany was also a revolutionary fighter. And since then, Hungarian writers and intellectuals have nearly always been deep in the country's politics. For a Hungarian writer to have served a term in prison for political reasons is as usual – and I suppose as inevitable – as is a Ph.D. for an American.

In 1956 it was the writers who first voiced the general unrest when they demanded the relaxation of party control and the return of Imre Nagy to power. The forum in which they expressed their views was called, significantly enough, the Petőfi Club.

PALÓCZI-HORVÁTH: For the last two centuries, in choice situations when history took a turn, it was always writers who were somehow in the lead. In impossibly difficult situations where the whole national life got into a cul-de-sac, then poets and writers felt compelled to say out loud what everyone knew.

A.A.: George Gömöri, a young Hungarian writer now doing research at Oxford, takes this up:

GÖMÖRI: In Hungary the idea of a poet is something totally different from the idea of a poet in England or in any Western country. In Hungary a poet should express the desires, expectations, demands of the nation as such. In a way, you could say the poet is the exponent of these desires and ideas. Now this has been a pattern from the so-called reform age, from the early nineteenth century onwards. Petőfi, Ady, and Attila József, all these poets kept on this idea and produced poems which were not simply valuable as works of art and as '*poésie pure*' but were also very important in expressing the social and national problems. For instance, Attila József demanded social reforms and wrote about such problems as unemployment with some force. I think nobody, or very few people, did this in Western Europe. Generally speaking, this tradition was kept up even after the war. Ferenc Juhász was the last exponent of this idea of what you can call perhaps national romanticism in poetry.

A.A.: This poetic mixture of politics and romanticism is curious and peculiarly Hungarian. For the romanticism is not just the kind that goes with any young nationalism, sharpened and made even more idealistic by oppressive occupation. It's also romanticism in a more traditional, more personal sense.

BOLDIZSÁR: We are very proud of our lyrics, and we personally believe that our lyrical poets are as important as Bartók or Kodály in music. But we just can't translate them. For instance, we have four very great lyrical poets: Petöfi in the nineteenth century, Ady at the beginning of our century, Attila József who was a contemporary of mine – he died twenty years ago – and Radnóti, who was the youngest of them and was killed by the Nazis in '44. All four of them were lyrical poets in, let's say, the English sense of the word, but at least half of their verses are political verses which are inspired by national passions, by national ideas, by tradition.

Let's quote for instance – in English naturally – Ady, who wrote 'I was very much troubled by money, by blood, but there were only two things which really interested my poet's pen: politics and love'. Love and politics: these two are, in both Ady's and in Petöfi's poetry, so interwoven you can't say this is a love poet, this is a political poet, because the two are together. In Radnóti also; his best anti-German, anti-Nazi poems are love-letters to his wife.

A.A.: Hungarian writers, then, possess this curious ability to feel lyrically about politics. Endre Ady, for example, is the only poet who managed in the same poems to be both a full-scale Symbolist, in the manner of Verlaine and Rimbaud, *and* a political poet. To feel lyrically about politics – which I suppose was one of the elements of the '56 affair – has, as its balancing opposite, the flair for feeling political about love – which is the perennial element of cynicism in the Hungarian make-up.

This way of taking one's personal life with intense seriousness and other people's with considerable scepticism may be due to the mixture of the Romantic and Jewish heritages. But in Hungary there is no other. Unlike English or French poets, the Hungarians have never fought the battle between classicism and romanticism. They have no Ben Jonson, no Pope, no Racine. Their classics of literature are all Romantics: Petöfi, Arany, and their contemporaries. So perhaps the Marxism of someone like Lukács is important in their literature because, with its canons of realism and dialectic, it tries to impose an intellectual order, a kind of classicism, on their instinctive romanticism.

GÖMÖRI: Even in Attila József's poetry, there is a strong classicist strand and this is due to the fact that he somehow put his romanticism – or if you like forced his romanticism – into the rationalistic framework of Hegelian Marxist dialectic. And later on there was only one poet who came up to this, whom I would call a classicist in the Western sense of the word; that is Radnóti. Radnóti died during the war – he was shot by the Germans – and he's certainly a very good poet. Now in his poetry, it was Marxism, partly Marxism but also partly Catholicism which worked as a classicizing factor.

A.A.: I doubt if Marxism essentially represents anything more 'classical' in Hungarian art than a kind of dull, immovable stone on which to blunt their instinctive romanticism. But it certainly encourages them in their general dislike of the new. Despite the Hungarian geniuses – Bartók and Kodály, Attila József, Sándor Weöres, Ferenc Juhász – Hungarian culture as a whole seems resistant to new forms, new styles.

Just as Latin remained the official language about five hundred years longer there than anywhere else in Europe, so Hungary has, in literature at least, always been reactionary, always a bit behind the times. Ady, for instance, is their great Symbolist poet. But he was a Symbolist about fifty years after the movement swept the rest of Europe. In literary matters, Hungary is a kind of Oxford of Europe, a home of lost causes. Péter Nagy described this when he said:

NAGY: I think in a way for literature, for the stage and so on, the ethical norms have been laid down by Petöfi, Arany and their followers, in the sense that the styles which were chic in the forties and fifties of the last century are prevailing still in the taste of the general public.

A.A.: In the offices of *Nagy Világ*, an excellent magazine devoted entirely to presenting foreign literature in translation to the Hungarian public, Gabriel Mihalyi, a young critic who works there as editor, reluctantly agreed that there is a resistance to new forms in art:

MIHALYI: There are two sorts of resistance. There is a sort of *petit-bourgeois* resistance, *petit-bourgeois* feelings and thinking and morals; but there is also some real and some founded resistance to *avant-garde*ism, because we don't agree with all that is done in *avant-garde*ism – with the unrealistic and sometimes too morbid tendencies. I think there is some real criticism from our public and sometimes they are right when they criticize *avant-garde*ism. They want to know it and it is necessary that we should present *avant-garde* works to them. And I think sometimes they are wrong in criticizing – when they don't understand it – but sometimes they are right, because they have a natural and accurate feeling that something is quite alien to them.

A.A.: It is, in short, more than usually hard to separate art and morals in Hungary. The resistance to new art forms has its ethical parallel: a certain official moral primness.

NAGY: On the surface, I wouldn't say the official, but the accepted pattern is the Victorian norm of sexual and social life.

44

A.A.: There was a perfect example of this in action when I was in Budapest. One of the national theatres was performing *A Streetcar Named Desire*. And miraculously transforming it. Had I not known beforehand, I would never have guessed that the theme of the play and the trouble with the heroine was sexual. In Budapest she was merely suffering from the excesses of unrequited romantic love. This of course is merely a trivial instance of something which Palóczi-Horváth says is general in Eastern Europe:

PALÓCZI-HORVÁTH: I might be mistaken but I detect a moral primness all over the western communist world. By that I mean the Soviet Union and the European satellites. Reading magazines, and mainly the literary magazines of young writers, I seem to feel or even see that moral primness there too.

A.A.: Well, the primness is perfectly understandable. The social revolution in Russia, in Poland and in Hungary involved lifting the countries by their bootstraps out of near-feudalism into the industrial twentieth century. There is every reason why the morality should lag behind the technical sophistication, and also every reason why it should officially have been encouraged to do so: the process of industrialization has meant too much effort, too much self-sacrifice and general deprivation of ease to allow for much latitude elsewhere in behaviour.

But the industrial revolution has also gone hand in hand with a cultural revolution. So the real and difficult question is how deep does this cultural change go? Or rather, there are two questions. First, if *petit-bourgeois* habits of taste have remained more or less the same for a hundred years, what genuine effect has the vast cultural revolution had? Second, if the moral primness is only a public surface, is the passion for culture much more than that?

But what is this cultural revolution? Gömöri describes it sceptically:

GÖMÖRI: As far as the Hungarian régime's cultural policy is concerned, I believe that quite a great advance has been made in the field of literacy, a great many more books have been published in the last eight years than ever before in Hungary; a great number of people are reading who never took a book in their hands before. All the same, this is only an achievement in quantity. It's not very much of a qualitative achievement. By which I mean that general standards, general aesthetic standards of people, are still very much nineteenth-century standards.

A.A.: The apparent achievement, however, is extraordinary. And this is not only a question of the proliferation of extremely well-equipped cultural centres, with their own libraries, theatres, lecture halls, dance halls, and their evening classes in everything. It is also a matter of the sheer increase in reading. The official figures are staggering. Book-publishing increased four hundred per cent between 1938 and 1954. In 1961, an average of sixty-one forints a head was spent in buying books throughout the country; and books are both beautifully produced and very cheap – as low as three forints each. Of these only twenty-three per cent of the purchases was by libraries. In Budapest each year the population as an average consumes fourteen books a head: seven bought, seven from libraries. Every morning after the seven o'clock news, three new books are officially recommended. Culture has become a kind of national pursuit. István Vas, the poet, gives a couple of examples of this:

ISTVÁN VAS: We have published Shakespeare; there was a new edition of two thousand copies. It was sold I think in two years. After that we had a new edition in '55 of ten thousand copies. It was sold in one year. And now this year we have published the third edition of the same translation in thirty-five thousand copies, which is enormous in Hungary. You must always consider that we are ten millions, not quite ten million.

I have translated Apollinaire too, a little volume during the war, which was published in five hundred copies. And it wasn't sold till the end of the war. After the war, after '56, we have published Apollinaire in two editions; I think it was in ten thousand or fifteen thousand copies. And it was sold in weeks, in weeks. And the public liked it.

A.A.: Even Paul Ignotus has to admit an improvement:

IGNOTUS: I think one never knows about these statistics. One has always to make some allowances for cosmetic touching-up operations about them. But I think that basically this trend does exist. First of all, the Communists did encourage reading. They did fight illiteracy. They preferred people to read. They had a very high respect for literary and other cultural values, which still stems from Lenin's time. Even the Stalinist régime at its peak had a strange admixture of reverence to or towards culture and a wish to read. Those writers accepted as good men – either from the point of the régime or as people whom the régime had to put up with in one way or another – were really very well treated. They were almost as well treated as a high party *apparatchik*, which means a lot, or as a company director in the national industries. They belonged to the new plutocracy.

A.A.: The official policy affects not merely the well-being of the writers: it goes right through Hungarian society. Everybody reads. The shops which sell books are as busy and as well-stocked as those selling food. And the books are all good books. The taxi-drivers waiting on the ranks read Stendhal, not Mickey Spillane. There is, of course, a simple reason for this: Mickey Spillane and company are not available, just as cowboy films are not shown. Indeed, when I suggested that some cowboy films are very fine as works of art I was thought to be making a sophisticated, decadent joke. There is, in short, a good deal of snobbery about the Hungarian culture-lust. Yet even snobbery, I suppose, can have good effects:

ISTVÁN VAS : I think snobbism is sometimes the beginning of culture. Of course, sometimes it is the ending of culture. But I think Hungarian snobbism, if we have it, is mostly the beginning of culture. You cannot trace a very strict limit between respect for culture and between snobbism.

A.A. : You can, however, trace a fairly strict line between respect for culture and real discrimination. My impression is that the majority of Hungarians are interested in culture the way some people are interested in money: what kind matters less to them than how much. I imagine those taxi-drivers have only a very muffled idea of why Stendhal is better than Spillane. And they probably don't much care.

All the same, they read him, undaunted by length or *longueurs*. And this is a colossal achievement in popular education. It is also part of the Hungarian temperament.

BOLDIZSÁR: I think the basic difference between an English reader and an Hungarian reader is that, for the English reader, literature is an aesthetic experience, an entertainment or pastime or something like that. For the Hungarian reader it is a national passion, part of the national existence.

A.A. : There is a saying that of the ten million people in Hungary, nine million are writers. Politically, this national passion may be the expression of something else.

PALÓCZI-HORVÁTH: Having limited private possibilities of freedom and a limited sort of life, and feeling fenced in, people have a very great craving to keep up with the world, to be at least culturally equal with more fortunate people.

A.A. : What I think this amounts to, in fact, is that in

Hungary, after all the horrors of the last two or three decades, music, literature, and the rest have become – despite their insistently political overtones – a substitute for politics. Perhaps all small countries, once they have been made by suffering to realize how small they are, aspire to the condition of Switzerland: that of comfortable neutrality. In Hungary this aspiration has been almost a mania. They wanted to become neutral in 1945 after fighting alongside the Nazis. They even had the same – and, in the circumstances, lunatic – dream in 1956.

PALÓCZI-HORVÁTH: Well, it's in Hungarian history, being put between two masses – the Germanic masses in the west and the Slavic–Russian masses in the east. For centuries our dream was always to stay neutral. If the two big people fight each other, the Germanic masses and the Slavonic masses, we should be out of it. This is a five-hundred- or six-hundred-years-old dream in Hungary: neutrality.

A.A.: Since '56, however, neutrality is no longer even a dream. The Hungarians are fairly and squarely in the Russian orbit. All that can be hoped in the realm of practical politics is for the present *détente* to continue, for Kádár to stick to his slogan: 'Those who are not against us are for us.' For the rest, at the moment, the living is easy and culture absorbing. It even looks as though, despite the Hungarian tradition, a passion for poetry need no longer automatically involve a passion for politics. As that novelist said to me, 'All I want is to be left in peace'. And lest you are tempted to feel self-righteous or complacent, he was defending himself as much against representatives of the West as against the Communists.

3. Czechoslovakia (1962)

When this was written it reflected fairly accurately, I think, the tone of the country at that time: a tone, above all, of considerable impatience with petty restrictions and shortages and stupidities. Soon after, however, the thaw began, and since then the process of liberalization has gone faster and farther than in any of the other countries I know in the Eastern bloc – *which is as it should be, given the solidly* bourgeois *habit of mind of the nation as a whole. The result is that although Czechoslovakia was in 1962 still the most Stalinist of the countries I visited, it is now the most easygoing and 'normal'. That oppressive air of gloom and resentment has vanished. Both good humour and the arts now thrive with remarkably little restriction.*

A.A.

*

As usual, it was quite different from what I'd expected. When you arrive in Warsaw or Budapest you find something totally alien, a way of living and thinking which is just out of focus, hard to adjust to, harder still to pin down. I innocently supposed that this was due to the new political structure of these countries, that communism, however willingly or unwillingly accepted, changed the whole national tone. Hence that it was the fundamental political transformation in the ways of thinking and living which had created that international rift which in turn created the Cold War.

After a couple of weeks in Prague I see now that I was wrong. Fundamentally, the Poles and Hungarians are alien more for what they are – in their make-up, their national temperaments – than for their politics. After all, Czechoslovakia is one of the most rigidly orthodox of all the Eastern European countries. The ruling élite may decry the cult of personality, but it remains as near Stalinist as makes no difference. Prague is thick with red stars, red flags, Russian propaganda. And many of the writers I met there were orthodox communists. This is very different from Poland, where Gomulka is – or was – liberal, subtle, not particularly dogmatic, rather Western in his political approach, and it is difficult, in any but official circles, to meet even a Marxist. Despite all this, the Czechs are closer to the Western democracies – particularly to small countries like Belgium – than the Poles, still less the Hungarians, could ever be.

They have that depressed, docile air you find so often in England, that slightly withheld manner of people who expect automatically to be disliked. But it goes deeper than that: it is a question of tradition, a tradition that goes back a good deal farther than the Communist *coup* of February 1948. The Czechs have a kind of realism which comes from the habit of democracy. For, essentially, democracy is an un-romantic affair; to have it you must worry less about your soul than about a decent, civilized way of life. So it tends to be associated with more practical religions like Protestantism or Judaism than with auto-cratic, soul-centred religions like Catholicism. It is also associated with industrialization, which assures enough general wealth to allow people to think about civilized living and the use of leisure. Finally, democracy presumes the habit of culture, a marked respect for the arts and scholarship spreading down through all levels of society.

All this the Czechs have – more or less. Their religious habits were dominated by John Hus, the disciple of Wyclif – who was a radical and successful reformer of the Church a hundred years before Luther.

The country has been heavily industrialized since the last century. As someone proudly informed me, there are more television sets in Czechoslovakia than in any European country except England and Western Germany; there is also a paid-up waiting list of ninety thousand for Skoda cars. As for the arts and sciences: Prague has been a great cultural centre since the reign of the Emperor Charles IV in the fourteenth century. When Petrarch visited it in 1356 he wrote:

I confess that nowhere have I found less barbarism and more humanism than at the Court of the Emperor and among the distinguished men surrounding him. They are truly outstanding and highly cultivated persons, whose gentle and pleasant behaviour is such that they might be sons of Greece.

Charles University is one of the oldest in Europe (it was founded in 1348). Kepler and Tycho Brahe worked there. And Prague itself – infinitely elegant, like a Baroque Christmas cake – was Mozart's favourite city and the home of Kafka, Rilke and Werfel.

Romantic, passionate nations like Poland, Hungary, and Russia produce revolutions, occasional geniuses, and a great deal of social injustice. In comparison, the Czechs are solid, industrious, settled and fair. They produce reformers like Hus, scholars like Comenius, and motor-cars.

The Czechs, then, are an efficient people and a cultured one. But somewhere in their development something went wrong: they lack the cohesive passion of nationalism. It is said that in order to be at their best they have to work for someone else: the Czech division fought superbly for the Russians, so did the Czech pilots in the R.A.F. But the Czech Army itself has scarcely ever won a battle.

The breaking-point, I suppose, was the defeat of the Czechs by the Habsburgs at the Battle of the White Mountain in 1620. It made a kind of hole in the national history. After it the property of most of the nobility was confiscated and sold off to Habsburg supporters – Austrian, German, Italian and Spanish. The nobles themselves and the burghers were offered the choice of religious conversion or exile. Catholicism became the state religion and German the state language. And the Habsburg empire lasted for three hundred years – until 1918.

The result was a cultural paradox. The Habsburgs transformed Prague into the great Baroque showpiece of

Europe at the same time as they forced indigenous Czech culture underground. The arts became a foreign import, mostly in a foreign language. Native Czech work, from being cosmopolitan and sophisticated, became more or less folk art. Not entirely, however, as Aloys Skoumal, one-time Cultural Attaché in London, points out:

SKOUMAL: Until recently that particular period, the Baroque period, was regarded as an absolute blank. Recent studies seem to show that there was a continuous stream of poetry going on at that time, poetry perhaps not first-rate but still rather important, which later on, during the revival period, influenced Mácha, Erben, and many others.

A.A.: Scholarship may have recently unearthed links between the flourishing Czech culture of the seventeenth century and the Renaissance of the nineteenth, which was led by the poet Mácha. But the practical effect of the Habsburg gap on the language was enormous. Defining it here is Jan Werich, actor, comedian, writer, director, and one of the most popular figures in contemporary Czech culture:

WERICH: During those years, those three hundred years, other things happened. I think that, for instance, the English language – that was Shakespeare at the beginning of the seventeenth century – the English language grew up through the brains and the mouths of English people as such; I mean the nobility and the common people as well. But here, here in our country, the educated people and nobility spoke German, and just the people spoke Czech and were sort of guarding the Czech language. If you knew Czech, you would find in it all the small things of daily life, you know, like earth and brooms. I mean folk poetry and such stuff is beautiful, it's nice, as long as you speak about concrete things. But it's very hard in Czech to speak about abstract things – which is very easy in French or even in English – because there is that lag of three hundred years. Then in the last century, a hundred years ago, there were people in our country, Czechs, who were called 'wakers-up', intellectuals and mostly well-meaning people who wanted to save the Czech language and the Czech spirit. They invented words, and they took over vocabulary from the Slav languages, from Russian and so on, so that the Czech language would be able to express itself in abstracts too. That was done only one hundred years ago, but it's really an achievement, because nowadays in the Czech language you can speak even in abstracts, abstracts about everything. But it wasn't like this a hundred years ago. And that wakening-up of the Czech spirit was something really very surprising.

A.A.: This waking-up of the Czech language and cultural life a hundred or so years before the final dissolution of the rule of the Habsburgs meant that when the country finally got its independence in 1918 it was ready for full-scale modern democracy. Both the arts and industries were thriving. So, unlike Poland and Hungary, Czechoslovakia did not have to be dragged protesting into the twentieth century. Between 1918 and 1938, when the Nazis marched in, Czechoslovakia was a model of liberal, Western-style democracy. Both the Presidents between the two wars, Masaryk and Beneš, were university professors. The arts flourished. Extremely sophisticated experiments were carried out in pure poetry by a group who called themselves the 'Poetists' and by the 'Structuralist' critics. Inevitably, the country looked west for its impetus in the arts and politics. But this, according to Professor Otakar Vočadlo, one-time head of the English Department at Charles University, was part of an old Czech tradition:

VOČADLO: That sympathy with the English way of thought is very striking, I think, for a people who are living in the middle of Europe. Our greatest people – I mean representative men like John Hus or Comenius and right down to Masaryk – they all found English literature and English thought very congenial. I need hardly mention

Wyclif. John Hus simply adored him, and the whole Hussite movement was under Wyclif's influence. Then an Englishman came over, Peter Payne was his name; we called him Master English. Well, he was one of the Hussites. He went to the Council of Basle as one of them. There was mutual understanding between Hus's followers and the Lollards. Their leader, Sir John Oldcastle, who degenerated into Jack Falstaff, was in correspondence with our Hussites. If you think of the distance and all the obstacles in the way, it's very striking. Or take, for instance, John Amos Comenius – Komenský as we call him – the educationalist. He was invited to England. He was a disciple of Bacon, and John Pym, 'the uncrowned King' of the Commons, was his patron. He was patronized by quite a number of famous Englishmen – for instance by the learned John Selden and Robert Boyle – and the idea was that he should stay in England as the head of a sort of Solomon's house, a truly Baconian idea. England was to be the centre of world education. That's the idea which appealed to H. G. Wells so much.

And then we could go on. For instance, the great historian of Bohemia, Palacký, who created, as it were, the modern Czech feeling for the national identity. He started his history of the Bohemian people after reading Robertson of Scotland. And there are other influences which are equally striking. The beginning always seems to be England, whether it's Wyclif or later Sir Walter Scott. Scott and Shakespeare have influenced all our historical fiction and drama. We were very historically minded, which was only natural in a nation which had been submerged for so long; we had to live on our glorious past in order to keep our self-respect. It was difficult after 1918 in the so-called pragmatist generation, but they too looked chiefly to England for inspiration. Karel Čapek is a case in point. He is well known, probably best known of our modern writers, in England. His plays are Wellsian or Shavian if you like, and he loved English literature. He called it 'a diamond field', meaning those influences which were so fertile in our country. It was due to him that I started forty years ago the collection of modern English classics which I called The Standard Library. It had a very great success.

A.A.: But, thanks to the Chamberlain government, all this was altered. Petr Pujman of the Writers' Union describes what happened:

PUJMAN: Then came the year 1938 and the Munich crisis. You cannot imagine what the Munich crisis meant as far as the psychology and mentality of the Czech nation is concerned. It meant a terrible disillusion and a complete collapse of faith in the Western powers. I could perhaps tell you four lines of one of the poems by one of our most outstanding poets of that time, František Halas. Of course, I can give you only the word-by-word English translation, not a poetic one; it's approximately:

> Strikes, strikes the bell of treason,
> The bell of treason.
> Sweet France, proud Albion.
> And we loved them both.

This poem really expresses the feelings of the nation very exactly. Then after Munich came a great renewal of faith in Russia. And together with it came also the attitude of the Communist Party during the Munich crisis, because the Communist Party at that time was really the only party which was uncompromisingly in favour of resisting the Nazi threat and fighting against them. Then of course the moral influence of the Soviet Union rose immensely also during the times of the war. And then came the year 1945, with the arrival of the Red Army in Prague. So all these things taken together and taken into consideration might explain perhaps a little the true nature of the relations between the Soviet Union and Czechoslovakia.

A.A.: This feeling for Russia was not, however, a new thing. Since Czechoslovakia, unlike Poland, had had no direct experience of Russia – they had no border in common, for example – Russia had remained an alternative ideal to the West.

PUJMAN: I think it ought to be said that the feelings of friendship for Russia go very deep back into our history, because already towards the end of the eighteenth century and during the nineteenth century, when the national revival of the Czechoslovak nation took place, Russia was always considered, unlike in Poland and Hungary, by all our leading patriots as the possible liberator of the Czechs from the Habsburg yoke. The Czech nation didn't have such a bad experience with Tsarist Russia as, for instance, Poland had. We developed a kind of Pan-Slavonic feeling and always hoped that Russia might be the liberator who would unite all Slavs in a great brotherhood of Slavonic languages, thus freeing them from the German and the Habsburg oppression. This feeling remained till the twentieth century. Of course, it was of a slightly different character then, because after 1918, when the first Czechoslovak independent state was formed, we didn't have to deal with Russia any longer but with the Soviet Union. Czechoslovakia, as you will know, was already before the war quite a highly industrialized country with a very strong working class; and it had a liberal *bourgeois* régime, a democratic régime where the Communist Party was legal and had its own Press, had its own very strong intelligentsia. On the other hand, the official politics were orientated, as you well know, towards France and England, and France and England had also very strong ties of friendship in the feelings and minds of the Czechoslovak nation.

A.A.: The speaker, of course, is a Marxist. But he is on to a real truth. Despite Stalinism – and that is a large despite – the Communist Party still has a certain emotional hold in Central Europe because of its solid and consistent opposition to the Nazis. This raw nerve – the fear of Nazism – is carefully played on by the party leaders. Everywhere there are reminders of Nazi atrocities, everywhere warnings against the rearmament of Western Germany. Much of this seems to me, personally, to be quite justified. But it can become ridiculous. Reading the official *Outline of Czech History* you would never know that England and America fought *against* Hitler: the implication is that they were merely playing games to encourage him to attack Russia. The Nazi–Soviet pact is not mentioned.

But this has a practical effect both on the arts and on the emotional climate of the country. Indeed, the basic difference between Eastern Europe and the West is in the form the general nervousness takes, the sources, as it were, of the national paranoia. The whole of the Soviet *bloc* is still transfixed by the last war, by the inhuman atrocities and economic devastation wrought by the Nazis. And the Communist Party fastens on to this, endlessly nagging, as though it were its only *raison d'être*. In the West, on the other hand, we are paralysed by the thought of the *next* war, by the prospect of atomic atrocities and devastation. In the communist countries no one seems either aware or even interested in the atomic threat; nuclear disarmament is simply one side of the game of international politics.

Hence when a war novel comes out in the West it tends to be about the horrors of war as such – like *Catch 22* – whereas in the East it's about the sufferings under the Nazis. Some of it is very good; for example, Arnošt Lustig's two brilliant collections of short stories mostly about Jewish boys in the concentration camps. Much of it is less good. But all of it is successful. For instance, Jan Otčenášek's *Romeo, Juliet and the Darkness* is a rather tiresome, sentimental little novel. But it has all the right ingredients: a tragic love affair between a Czech youth and a Jewish girl played out against a background of the Nazi occupation and the death of Heydrich. As a result it has sold vastly, been translated into nineteen languages and made into an opera.

The last war, in short, is still central to Czech experience. For example, the very intelligent critic, František Vrba uses war experience certainly as a way of distinguishing between the generations and also, he seems to imply, as a means of critical discrimination when he discusses the leading middle-generation poet, Miroslav Holub, and the very young Josef Hanzlík:

VRBA: They represent a different feeling for life. Holub was born, if I am not mistaken, in 1923 and he began to write when he was about thirty or so. He and his contemporaries – Šotola or Šiktane or Diviš – are the generation who went through the war. They were adults when the war came and they knew already what it was all about. I do not know how to translate it now, but Šotola has a beautiful verse that says: 'The war is like broken glass in our arteries and in our blood.' And this broken glass, these particles of broken glass, are always hurting and itching. While the young people, young fellows like Hanzlík, they are the generation born around the thirties and they didn't go through this experience. They went through another experience. At first they were educated and entered a society which was beginning with great difficulty to build socialism – with all the contradictions and difficulties which arose with the transition from the period of the cult of Stalin to the present return to the Leninist practice. And they feel it very, very strongly. Now their main idea is of acute responsibility for this world of ours, by which I mean of the world they are living in. Now, they too remember the war, for instance. They remember what Fascism meant, what the Nazi concentration camps meant, what the persecution of the Jews meant and so on. But they remember it not from direct experience like the people who are ten years older, but they remember it as children. For instance, Hanzlík has written a very beautiful poem in which he remembers when he was six and on their street in the town where he lived a Jewish girl of his age was taken away by the Nazis. Now this remembrance from childhood made a very strong impression on his feelings. From this, I would say, stems the feeling of responsibility for a peaceful world.

A.A.: Note how the idea of peace – that is, of the next war – is thrown in as an afterthought. But Vrba's comment has two implications. First, the middle generation of Czech poets, who were already mature as writers during the bad Stalinist period, are nearly all staunch Communists, many of them party members; while the younger generation, still in their twenties, are involved less with politics than with the business of finding their own poetic identities.

PUJMAN: If we were to talk about the present state of our poetry, we would have also to compare it a little with what it was, say, ten years ago. At that time the chief problem in our poetry, as well as in our prose, was 'Socialism: yes or no? Capitalism: yes or no?' These questions do not appear any longer in our literature, neither in the poetry nor in the prose, because socialism is quite a matter of course for everybody, for the older generation as well for the younger one. So that it's quite natural that the development of our poetry turns now to more intimate problems and to ethical problems and to the problems of conscience as well.

I would say the chief question now is, 'How to act in a socialist society?' This implies also the question of conscience. That is to say, that your actions, all your deeds, all you say must be in perfect harmony with your conscience so that you can come to a full development of your individuality; and in this respect you can become also a good socialist.

A.A.: This ethical conflict in the poets may have loud political reverberations but it is also a question of poetic form. Speaking of the youngest generation, Aloys Skoumal said this:

SKOUMAL: What in my view binds them all together is an absolute integrity. Very often they seem rather sober poets. They are absolutely unpathetic, but what they do is something which they try to do with all their heart and with all their force. It seems there is a good deal, not of aversion, but a good deal of opposition towards what the preceding generation of Czech poets stood for. I mean as regards form.

A.A.: You might say that the end of the cult of personality in politics was the beginning of opportunity for the *artists* to cultivate *their* personalities. But this question of form belongs to a poetic argument which was part of the Czech literary tradition long before political commitment became an important criterion.

VRBA: I would say that Czech poetry had a very, very stressed lyrical strain – of roses and nightingales and so on and so forth. Even a good poet like Seifert, for instance, who is a contemporary of Holan and Nezval, is sometimes the soft poet of lyrical moods and so on.

Holub now introduces thought. He is against all lyricism, he attacks the poets of roses and nightingales and such stuff: he's for pure thought in his poetry. Among the contemporary readers, there are many people who object to his poetry; they say it's just a skeleton of pure ideas. Personally, I find this poetry very stimulating in the present environment, because it's something like a national disease to be very lyrical.

I would say that there are two tendencies in contemporary or modern Czech poetry, beginning in the twenties. One is represented in the first place by Nezval who would be something in the vein of Whitman, of Mayakovsky; the broad world, everything comes into his poetry and finds its lyrical expression. Then there is a second line represented by František Halas, who was the opposite of Nezval, who tried to be very concise, to use as few words as possible. He was a poet of moral conflicts within modern man, while Nezval was the poet of the big conflicts, of the, so to speak, cosmic conflicts of the modern age. In this sense Holub is a disciple of Halas, because he tries in his best poems – and sometimes a poem means just a few lines – he tries to condense as much meaning as he can into a few words.

A.A.: What are these poems of Holub's like? Here is one of his shortest and best-known pieces, *A Helping Hand*:

> We gave a helping hand to grass –
>   and it turned into corn.
> We gave a helping hand to fire –
>   and it turned into a rocket.
> Hesitatingly
> Cautiously
> We give a helping hand
> to people,
> to some people –

The form is free (the formal influences are probably the Polish poet Rózewicz and the American William Carlos Williams), but the intellectual movement is precise, ironical and analytic. This fits with Holub's professional life. For he is not a full-time poet. He is a pathologist engaged in theoretical medical research. Here he is speaking of his two activities and of how his habit of scientific analysis influences his poetry:

HOLUB: As a scientific worker I have to analyse everything, every fact and every word, and I can't be satisfied with a normal, with a current interpretation of things. The same thing applies to my poetry. I would like not to end with words, with terms, but I would like to analyse them, to go more deeply under the face of reality. This may be the whole problem of intellectual poetry: not to write about the world – how it seems, how it has been described for centuries – but to go deeper, to try to bring new basic facts about things which are up to now just described from a visual impression, from the emotive parts. I deal with emotions analytically, emotions as themes for poems.

Of course, you have your own emotions – even scientific

workers, I think, have normal emotions – but this is like fuel, like a motor, for the poem. But the content, the form of a poem, this is formed by the more analytical programme.

A.A. : Although Holub himself claimed kinship with the American Beat poets (largely, it struck me on, the ground that they all dislike ex-President Eisenhower), Vrba compared him to T. S. Eliot. This seems much nearer the mark. Despite the immense differences in politics, formalism and stature, Holub, like Eliot, has the analytical habit of mind. Though this analysis works within the canons – though not according to the rules – of Marxist realism, he is also a highly original poet and, in his own way, he works within the Czech tradition of experiment. He has, in fact, been experimenting with realism itself.

HOLUB : One of the questions here we feel very deeply is the question of being understood by as many people as possible. So I thought once that we should try to publish poetry in another way, not as closed books composed only of poems but as books with photographs or pictures or, say, with music. So I am trying now to make some books with modern photographs. I happened to encounter a young photographer who has photographed, in a very modern way, life in a hospital and a laboratory. This is very close to my own experiences, and so I found it, before I started, very easy to write poems in some way connected with his photographs, not illustrating, but just connected, just starting from the level where the photograph ends, so to speak. Usually the photographs come first and I write the poems after seeing the photographs, not describing the photograph but going on from the photograph; I hope going farther than the photographs, or behind them.

A.A. : The results are impressive. And they are not isolated. This attempt to fuse one art with another is being carried out by several artists in Czechoslovakia. Indeed it has even affected the equivalent of Home Service broadcasting, as Karol Reif, Head of the Foreign Relations Department of the Czechoslovak Radio explained to me:

REIF: What we are striving towards is to attain well-composed programmes. Perhaps an example would serve our purpose best: a few weeks ago I had an evening programme which consisted mainly of poetry by a Soviet poet following one of Mozart's deepest and most serious, non-Mozart-like symphonies. And although these two items came from various centuries, various cultural circles, together they gave a very good and very surprising effect of entity, of some inner conformity. This is what we are aiming at.

A.A.: The best known of these experiments in unifying the arts is the Magic Lantern, which has now been shown all over Europe. In principle, the idea of the Magic Lantern is brilliant. It is an attempt to bring cinema and theatre together in a kind of total entertainment. It uses a black stage and three cinema screens: a large one at the back of the stage, and two half-screens set at angles on either side. So it is possible, theoretically, to have on the same stage at the same time four different images of the one figure: that is, the live actor himself and three film versions of him. It is equally possible to have four completely different images interacting at the same time. The potentialities of this are enormous. Perhaps it could even end in a new form of entertainment. But to do so, it would, I think, have to go by way of abstraction – one of the Magic Lantern shows has, in fact already hovered on the edge of this. And there are two forces working against that. First, abstract art is still not officially recognized in proper Marxist circles. Secondly, the huge expense of mounting a Magic Lantern show – each one costs as much as forty productions at Prague's National Theatre – means that the commercial boys have a deafeningly loud say in the production. The result, as in so much cinema, is vulgarization. But that doesn't, essentially, detract from the brilliance of the original conception.

It is the brain-child of the one artist of undoubted international genius now working in Czechoslovakia: the stage designer Josef Svoboda. Single-handed he has brought about a revolution in the staging of plays. He has broken down the convention whereby the actors move more or less on one level against a fixed backdrop. In his productions the whole of the stage is used – all its depth and all its height, from the top of the proscenium arch to the floor. Instead of fixed backdrops he sets a scene by using, for example, a dozen or so little cinema screens suspended all over the stage space, each with its separate moving image. Instead of painted flats, he uses walls of light or narrow beams from specially designed spotlights reflected against black mirrors. He has, in every sense, broken down the walls of the conventional stage design. To do so, he told me, he learned physics in order to refute the experts who said his ideas were impossible. The state has given him his own school in which to train not only future designers but also technicians skilled enough to handle the delicate machinery his productions demand. After all, stagehands who both know about electronics and can read music are hard to find. As head of this school he can by-pass the bureaucracy of the usual state machinery and get what he wants done with the minimum of fuss. The results are startling.

It would seem that Svoboda has the freedom to give his originality its head for two reasons. First, unlike the other arts, the theatre is a collective effort. It is less obviously one man's responsibility and one man's vision than is, say, poetry. Svoboda himself seemed to confirm this when he described himself as an architect *manqué*. (He began his serious work during the Stalinist nadir of taste and, in his own words, 'I saw that in architecture I'd not be able to do what I wanted, so I turned to stage design.') The second reason is that the theatre is a form of mass entertainment –

and Svoboda helps to keep the great National Theatre consistently full. Therefore the complicated Marxist canons of realism do not apply.

For realism is the key term in the arts in all the communist countries. But in the face of the gradual liberalization which is taking place in the Kremlin, the meaning of the word is slowly being revised. In the bad old Stalinist days 'socialist realism' meant a non-imaginative – as it were, statistically correct – representation of reality, plus the edification derived from the spectacle of the positive hero with a positive attitude to socialism. Art, in short, had to serve the purposes of the party. There realism began and ended. It is now becoming a subtler and more flexible term. Consider, for example, the case of Kafka, who, although he wrote in German, was born and worked in Prague. Until recently he was simply ignored. Now he is coming back in – suitably revised to fit the magic formula.

VRBA: In the years before '56, he was a hot potato. We knew he was a great writer, but we didn't know what to do with him. Because we did not agree, and I say it for myself, I do not agree with him. My feeling of the world is different from Kafka's; I do not feel as though I'm in a Castle, shut in by bureaucracy, and so on. You know it by heart. Yet I consider Kafka to be a very great artist, a very great realist, who magnificently expressed the ideas and the feelings of people who feel like that. Just this year, a very interesting short picture called *The Double Trial* was shown in Bergamo in Italy, where it won the first prize in the category of documentary films. It is a film about Kafka. I think that this film is a little bit one-sided because it tried to link that feeling of anxiety and fear in Kafka with the presentiments of the coming fascism and war, and so on. I think this was really one-sided, but it's brought Kafka to the large audiences in Czechoslovakia. They are finally discovering that there was a great writer who lived among us, and his books are being published.

A.A.: But what works for Kafka doesn't necessarily work for less famous writers. The question of realism has recently come up in a strong form as the result of a speech made in Prague by the French Communist poet, Louis Aragon. He criticized the pressures put on writers to conform to a drab and rigid ideological pattern, and remarked at one point that literature must beware not only of the enemy on the right but also of the pirates on the left. The result is described by a student of Czech affairs:

MR Y: Well, there were many remarks about it but I think the most interesting one was carried in the official newspaper of the Writers' Union, the *Literary News*, by Kohout, a dramatic writer. It all concerned the question of the positive hero. Apparently Aragon was very critical about the positive hero being always too positive. Kohout wrote that they were always directed by the official line to go among the people and describe their lives, or use the figures of the people in their plays or novels. And when they really did this and all of a sudden wrote about people not being as ideal as the positive hero should be, well, they were criticized for it and told off. So actually what it came to was that Kohout's article concluded by asking for more freedom, or 'let us write what we feel like writing'. But anyway it ended up by the Editor-in-Chief of this *Literary News*, Rybák, answering him, telling him that he was completely wrong. If you read among the lines, it means that you can write what you feel like as long as it's all right on the ideological basis.

A.A.: This is not strictly accurate. Kohout had concluded that literary works which supply a tactical political need are often necessary, but, he added – and I quote – 'they cannot definitely replace permanently real literature, just as the best of annual reports cannot replace fundamental philosophical and economic works'.

Rybák, the Editor-in-Chief of *Literárni Noviny* – the Czech equivalent of the *Times Literary Supplement* –

replied by arguing sophistically that Aragon hadn't meant what he seemed to mean by his phrase 'the pirates on the left'. Rybák then went on to explain that a work of literature must still be positive in its attitude to socialism, even if the main character is not.

Now this squabble is not important in itself. But it is typical of the Czechs' rather double attitude towards the gradual liberalization of the arts. For every two steps forward there must be at least one official step back. Their view of the young Russian poet, Yevtushenko, shows what I mean. Like the Poles, they don't think much of him as a poet. But they are enormously impressed by his courage in saying what he does. Someone remarked to me: 'It only needs a slight change in the political climate and Yevtushenko would be –' and with his finger the speaker sliced significantly across his throat. In short, liberalization in Czechoslovakia is a cautious affair. Each gesture must be such that it can, if necessary, be translated back into an orthodox 'positive' ideology:

MISS X: Suddenly we read in the Czech papers that in Poland they have got a theatre called 'The Second Storey Theatre', or 'Under the Roof Theatre', or something like that. And there was a call in our newspapers for the young generation of actors and directors to create their own theatres with new ideas. Since that time, since four or five years ago, we had about three or four really progressive theatres – progressive in a sense that they write their own plays in a new way. They are sort of political musicals, their trend is critical towards deficiencies and certain kinds of situations which one can see in this country. But the criticism is positive, if you know what I mean. It tries to improve things. And these theatres are very much beloved by the young generation – that young generation that is very modern, that goes modernly dressed, you know. The girls have got their hair put up and their eyes painted all over and wear the sort of large sweaters and jumpers and short skirts, and so on.

A.A.: There is no doubt that the younger generation with their smart clothes, a bit of money in their pockets, good cafés to dance in, and excellent sophisticated jazz, are much better off than their predecessors; much less harried and obsessed by politics.

MR Y: Now that there has been a general liberalization of practically everything, those people who could not somehow voice their ideas or write novels of that kind are using this liberal moment. They are making full use of it actually by writing in that way, forgetting the daily troubles of work and so on and, as I said, being interested much more in the personal things.

A.A.: In short, propagandist writing will no longer do. The public is patently not interested in it and the party line has been modified accordingly.

PUJMAN: If a poet or a writer wants to build a name in our society he cannot do so by writing political slogans. He can become a real name only if he becomes a really good poet.

A.A.: As a result of this official easing-up, it seems that even the hallowed war-time Nazi themes are going. George Theiner, who translated Arnošt Lustig's stories, gives an example of the new trend:

THEINER: So far most of the literature here, most of the good stuff certainly, has been concerned with the occupation, with the partisans and with the war in general. Fortunately, there has been a change for the better. One or two recent novels deal with present-day life in Czechoslovakia as opposed to what happened fifteen or twenty years ago. I have in mind, for instance, a new novel by one of the best young Slovak writers, Mináč, which deals with a young building engineer. It's more or less a love story of a young building engineer and his girl against a background of present-day life in Slovakia. I think it's very well written as a novel. It's certainly one of the best things we've had in the recent four or five years. It takes a very critical attitude to present-day life in this country, but quite apart from that it certainly is a good piece of writing. I don't think the difficulty now is so much in getting it published as rather in getting it written. I think very few people write that sort of stuff and Mináč is to be congratulated on doing so.

A.A.: But the stuff *is* gradually getting written. The non-orthodox young poets are published widely and the doyen of the older generation – the poet Vladimír Holan, who put himself under a kind of self-imposed house arrest during the Stalinist period – is now courted by the literary magazines for poems. A new book of his is said, at last, to be in preparation. The same goes for the great Czech lyric poet, Jaroslav Seifert, who was at one time in disfavour for being not sufficiently in touch with contemporary reality. Igor Hájek of Dilia, the state literary and theatrical agency, discusses another *cause célèbre*:

HÁJEK: There was a writer named Škvorecký here. He published a book in '58 which was very sharply criticized. And I may say this was publicized all over the world, in all newspapers; I personally read it in *Le Monde*. In France there was published recently a history of modern European literature in which they say that Josef Škvorecký is one of the most talented authors in Czechoslovakia, but he published only one book and he's not been heard from since then. This is not true, to say the least. He has published very many stories and I think that he is one of the most, if you may use this word, preferred authors. He has not written a book of his own since then because the one he published was written when he was about twenty – he is about thirty-six or thirty-seven now – and it was really an old book. He is now concentrating on stories, I think, perhaps under American influence. He's a translator of American literature too. He has published many stories, some of them you would maybe think very critical of some aspects of our life. But he's encouraged to write more stories. He was editor of a large publishing house here; and as a matter of fact he took a leave of absence just to write more and to be able to devote more time to writing. I must say practically all that he writes has been published; they accept everything he submits for publication.

A.A.: Officially, then, everything is publishable. At the moment, for example, there is a great vogue for Beatnik poetry. So I asked Petr Pujman what would happen if Czechoslovakia produced a genuine Beat poet of their own, who opted out of society in favour of a totally private world.

PUJMAN: Such a poet could go on writing as he likes. He certainly would be criticized by our critics in our literary journals and magazines for not being interested in the fate of his society. He certainly would be criticized perhaps for a kind of egoism because he thinks only of himself and not of the others whom he is living with. But after this criticism nothing would happen at all and, if he chose, he could go on writing as he did before.

A.A.: Of course, whether or not he would choose to go on writing in a way that seemed to offer him small hope of being published, is another matter. To punish a writer it is not necessary to throw him into prison; you simply have to deny him an audience. I met at least one man who claimed that an unfavourable review in the party paper *Rudé Právo* had jeopardized his immediate chances of having another book published. On the other hand, literature being the cut-throat business it is, this might simply have been an example of the perennial phenomenon of the older, established generation clamping down on the younger, rising generation, but using political ideology to do so.

All the same, the force and prevalence of the ideology does encourage the habit of double-think: that is, you really come to believe what you have been told is true, even if you know that, in fact, it is not. And double-think goes very easily with the kind of accommodating cynicism which the Czechs – who are, after all, the nation of the Good Soldier Svejk – are particularly expert in. I met, for example, a couple of people connected with the flourishing Psychological Clinic, and asked them how they managed to work despite the fact that Freud is not officially recognized by the Marxists. One of them replied: 'The answer is simple. You practise Freud, call it Pavlov and hope for the best.' I suppose the same thing goes for literature. You cultivate your originality, call it realism and hope for the best. As someone said to me 'There's no real censorship. They never say "No". They only say "Yes".' But they manage it so that a direct 'No' is never provoked. And it is this slightly dishonest manipulation which is resented.

There is, I found, a good deal of discontent going about like the 'flu. But you must distinguish between discontent – and the Czechs, like the English, are expert grumblers – and the kind of deep unrest caused by massive abuse and injustice which ends in explosions like the Hungarian revolution. The real criticism in present-day Czechoslovakia is not against the system as such but against official stupidity. This stupidity takes many forms. There are the endless minor irritations caused by an officious bureaucracy: I met someone, for example, whose copy of the new English translation of the Bible had been confiscated by the customs police. And it's extremely difficult for an unofficial person to receive through the mail even a left-wing publication like the *New Statesman*. Or consider the question of English studies at Charles University: just after the war the English Department numbered one thousand students. During the Stalinist period this dropped to under fifty – revolutionary writers like Milton, I suppose, being possible sources of political contamination.

Now, fortunately, the department is again being allowed to expand and about a hundred students read English. In themselves none of these things are particularly important. But they are representative of a tiresome official meddling in private affairs which grates on the nerves of ordinary people and induces a kind of permanent depressed watchfulness, which is out of character in this rather friendly, beer-swilling nation.

Much more important, however, is the official stupidity which comes down from above. As I mentioned before, Czechoslovakia was already a wealthy, comfortable, industrialized twentieth-century country when it got its independence in 1918. Now it seems to be very near bankruptcy. The shops may be crammed with factory-made goods, but there is a constant shortage of agricultural products. A few months ago there was practically no meat to be had. When I was there, butter and cheese were almost unobtainable and, I was told, in the country districts there was milk only for the children. Everywhere there are queues. During the meat shortage, the lines outside the butchers began at four in the morning. No doubt some of these shortages are artificially induced.

MISS X : Just at this moment, I think, there is a shortage of butter and cheese and milk. I don't think it's really a shortage. I think it's because a rumour goes through Prague suddenly one day – I don't know where it comes from or anything – that there is going to be a shortage of butter, so every woman who works in the household goes and buys all the butter she sees in the shops: which means they buy it in the morning and in the evening there is no butter at all.

A. A. : But however artificial the shortages may in part be, they are also in part due to a stupid official rigidity. Obviously the agriculture of a highly industrialized country like Czechoslovakia is a fairly delicate affair. The party machine, however, has enforced a monolithic collectivization on the farmers which forces them to work according to a fixed bureaucratic pattern. And these collectives are, as often as not, run by party members who have got their jobs for political reasons and so know very little about the intricacies of farming. Since agricultural communities in every country are conservative and against change, the combination of bureaucratic action and resentful reaction has badly fouled up the economy. And unnecessarily so, for a more flexible attitude would doubtless make all the difference. The Poles, for example, have cut their losses and handed the collectivized land back to the peasants. Even in Russia a good deal of private enterprise is allowed within the limits of collective agriculture. But in Czechoslovakia rules are rules and dogma dogma. So the farming stays wholly collectivized and largely inefficient.

I know that economic problems do not really fall within the scope of this investigation. I mention this only as a significant example. For it's important to understand that when one talks of discontent in a communist country, one does not mean that the population wants to put the clock back on the social revolution – which is what our own propaganda machine implies. But they do want freedom from petty restrictions, petty tyrannies, petty dogmatism. And this is felt particularly strongly in Czechoslovakia – although it is, in comparison with other Iron Curtain countries, fairly well off – because the party's rigid orthodoxy seems all the more forced and unreal in contrast to the liberal Western-style democracy which the country was used to before 1938. What is resented, in short, is not the system but the petty-mindedness of an unpopular ruling *élite*. The bitterest remark I heard was by someone who said of the party zombies: 'They are all Baroque artists. They want to twist everyone to fit on to the pedestal of their own petty imaginations.'

But perhaps there *is* something rather plastic in the Czech natural temperament. They seem to take very easily to set patterns. In the Middle Ages they were one of the most highly civilized peoples in Europe. After 1620, under the Habsburg domination, they almost ceased to exist as a nation. Then, when they got their independence in 1918, they had twenty years of extreme liberal democracy. Following the communist *coup* in 1948 they went into a period of total Stalinist Marxism. I wonder if they haven't kept this Stalinist mould, while the rest of Eastern Europe has followed the Kremlin into a more liberal style of behaviour, for a paradoxical reason. That is, the Czechs have stayed Stalinist because, of all the communist *bloc*, they are the most *bourgeois*. They are, I mean, most rootedly adjusted to the habit of civilized, non-violent, non-vicious behaviour, to decent comfort and docile, grumbling acceptance of the given machinery of government. In short, if there is a superficial uniformity in their communism, it may well be a manifestation of their *bourgeois* conventionality and easy-goingness.

Certainly, within the system they try to arrange life well: they have the best beer in Europe, legalized abortions, no laws against homosexuality, and divorce costs £10. And where politics don't intrude, the arts remain extremely sophisticated: the jazz, for example, or Svoboda's magnificent stage designs, or the mime theatres, or the brilliant cartoon films of Trnka, who is a good deal more skilled and imaginative than Walt Disney. And even where politics are felt the habit of experiment continues. Holub, for example, uses his Marxism to experiment in evolving new forms of poetry. Above all, Stalin's vast statue, which used to loom over Prague, has been dismantled. The man-made mountain on which it stood sank by some fifty feet in the two weeks I was there. And this may be a symbol of the new optimism:

MISS X: All these things are being discussed openly everywhere. There is one thing that I, for example, am waiting for, and that is the new generation; the new generation is going to grow up quite differently from the old Communist generation up till now. The new generation will first of all grow up in definitely better surroundings. In schools, as you know, they get free food, free books and pencils, and all things like that free. The economic situation of the new generation will be quite different. Therefore the sort of line of the development of the communist idea will be quite differently understood by them.

A.A.: What, in short, the Czechs are looking forward to is not the restoration of old styles but a new liberal, undogmatic stage of their Marxism. Jan Werich, who at all levels remains one of the most popular personalities in the country, sums it all up:

WERICH: I was introducing some recordings on the radio the other day and I said, speaking about progress, that it's not the people who are making progress but progress which is making people – meaning that progress is a deed of nature which has to come, as night follows day and day follows night. It belongs to nature and it makes the people. But it's not made by the people, the way some people are trying to tell us, because everything is progressive in nature, everything. The flowers in the room or in the garden, everything wants to be better than the last year, because that's the law of nature.

4. Yugoslavia (1963)

THE first problem is to know what country you are talking about. For the tourist the answer is simple: Yugoslavia means the beautiful Dalmatian coast with its islands and monasteries, old cities and modern resorts, its drama festivals and links with the Italian Renaissance and Venice. It means sun, swimming, sea-food, and a bit of quaint poverty to off-set the chic hotels. But go inland one hundred and twenty miles or so from Trieste and you are in Zagreb, which is pure Austrian – with all that implies of slightly fussy elegance, cream cakes, and the pervasive smell of coffee. Orson Welles chose it for the location shots of his film of Kafka's *The Trial*. South and east from there is Belgrade, a noisy modern town, flat as a cow pat on the plain, whose ugliness is gradually being modified by some fine modern buildings after the school of Mies van der Rohe. South again from there, an hour's flight, is Skopje, capital of Macedonia, where the ambitious beginnings of a new industrial city jostle with an old Turkish town: mosques, minarets, and bazaars, where the women wear baggy trousers, the men fezes, and the narrow streets are lined with the shops of silver-workers and sandal-makers.*

Which Yugóslavia? It's a question which even the Yugoslavs find difficult to answer, as Tomislav Ladan, a literary critic from Zagreb, says:

LADAN: We use the term Yugoslav culture and Yugoslav literature, but it should be understood in a geographical and political sense, because as a matter of fact we have several individual cultures incorporated in the term

* Or rather, they were. A few weeks after I was there, the town was shattered by an earthquake. The pictures showed the devastation to the apparently solid modern buildings. What must have happened to the flimsy old quarter scarcely bears imagining. I have not been back.

Yugoslavia and Yugoslav culture. That is, Macedonian, Croatian, Serbian, Slovenian, Montenegran and Bosnian and Herzegovinian. There are also three languages: Slovenian, Serbo-Croat, and Macedonian.

A.A.: Like most Eastern European states, the country we now call Yugoslavia did not emerge as a political entity until 1918, and even then it had another name. It was called the 'Kingdom of the Serbs, Croats and Slovenes'. This was only changed to Yugoslavia – the country of the South Slavs – by the royal dictator, Alexander, in 1929. And even that was not enough to hold the different nations together. Witness Jovan Hristić, a poet and critic from Belgrade:

HRISTIĆ: One of the main reasons why the old Yugoslav state – I mean the Yugoslav state in between the two world wars – went to pieces at the very moment of the German attack in 1941, was the fact that the government and the ruling class were not able to cope with the infinite complexity of national differences and national cultural traditions existing on the territory of Yugoslavia. In their policy they were bound to hurt this or that national pride.

A.A.: These national antagonisms continued at least until 1945. During the German occupation the Četniks, under their Serbian royalist leader, Mihailović, fought the partisans under Tito, a Croat communist. The Nazis set one ethnic and religious group against another and appalling atrocities were committed in the name of heaven knows what local patriotisms, racialisms, and plain antagonisms. But out of this, the beginnings of unity came. The Second World War and the German occupation were a common national trauma. This, in turn, created a common cause and a kind of common anti-trauma: I mean, the extraordinary heroism of the Partisan fighters, who have the same sort of patriotic emotional appeal as the Battle of

Britain pilots have here. They have helped create a unifying national bond.

The bond is still not perfect. I met Croats in Macedonia, and Montenegrans in Serbia, who talked as though they were exiled in some foreign and slightly inferior country; occasionally they even had trouble with the language. One wit suggested to me that Tito managed to keep the centre of government in the relatively less prosperous Serbian Belgrade not merely by personal genius but because he is a Croat. That way he satisfies the two dominant racial groups.

Be that as it may, it's certain that Tito's idiosyncratic brand of communism is based, above all, on the desire to create an efficient modern state from a collection of very different, often antagonistic nations, cultures and ethnic groups, speaking at least three separate languages. The problem, after the devastation of the last war, was not just to industrialize a rather backward country, but also to instil a temperamental and politically ill-educated people with a sense of responsibility – a sense, as it were, of having the vote, even in a one-party system. Hence Tito's brilliant solution of decentralized communism.

Unlike the Russian Communists, when Tito spoke of the state 'withering away' he acted as though he meant it. In modern Yugoslavia each republic is autonomous, although answerable to the federal government; so too is each factory, which functions as a competitive unit, run by workers' councils elected by the workers themselves. An American has described it as 'an indirectly controlled market economy, with elements of Keynesianism as well as of Marxism'. Thus the various national prides and rivalries are channelled into economic competition, which at the same time produces in the workers something of that sense of self-respect which is the basis of political responsibility.

That, anyway, is the theory. How well it has worked out in practice is not my business here. But what is happening in Yugoslavia economically and politically is also affecting all levels and areas of culture. For example, the head of the philosophy faculty at Belgrade University is Professor Mihailo Marković, a logician who wrote his doctorate under the supervision of Professor A. J. Ayer. He is, in short, adept in the Oxford brand of positivist philosophy. Yet when I asked him about current philosophy in Yugoslavia, he replied in this way:

MARKOVIĆ: For several years we had quarrels between dogmatists and revisionists, but most of the dogmatists here, as everywhere in my opinion, are not creative people; that's why they can be dogmatists. Hence so-called revisionists keep most of the important positions in our universities. And nobody calls them revisionists, in fact.

Philosophy has at least three important functions. One function is to give a general picture of the world, using all existing knowledge and sciences, and making generalizations from human practice in a given epoch. Another function is to elaborate epistemology and logic, to build up instruments which should be used in order to establish truth, to reach genuine knowledge. And then a third function is to express ideals of a given community in a given time, to say something about what life should be and what kind of society man should live in. This is not a political problem. This is a much more fundamental problem. One should take into account the particular situation in which man lives in a given time. Then also one should take into account the general picture of what man is, which means that one should make generalizations on psychology, sociology, social anthropology, and so on. And then on the basis of this objective knowledge one could establish which are the objective possibilities in a given society in a given time. Only then could one say, in an objective scientific way, which ideals have a chance to be accepted. At this point the moment of choice comes, because we always have more than one alternative, and we have to choose which one. For example, in our country – which is a rather underdeveloped country – should we just try to develop our technology as much as possible, neglecting all these by-products of excessive technicalization, or shall we do something now already to avoid these various forms of human degradation and dehumanization which is so evident in other developed industrial countries?

A.A.: This is not quite such a theoretical problem as it sounds, for it turns up, implicitly but continually, in literature as well as in philosophy and politics. It can be seen in its clearest and most basic form in Macedonian culture. Macedonia, as a separate national, political, and cultural entity, has existed for less than twenty years – only since after the last war. That it exists at all is probably due less to ethnic pressures than to international politics: it's an insurance against the territorial claims of Bulgaria and Albania. Before that Macedonia was, for five hundred years, an oppressed, primitive part of the Ottoman empire. And the Turks didn't move out until 1912. Mira Šunjić, Professor of English at Skopje University, takes up the story:

ŠUNJIĆ: As a consequence of the Turkish invasion that reached as far as Vienna, the Dark Ages of the Turkish rule intervened to wipe out all written tradition. This tide has been slow in retreating from this part of the world. Centuries passed, times when physical survival was of supreme importance. The old traditional folk-songs and stories were the only expression of the emotional reaction of this people to the world of cruel realities. Those who came out on top – the Turks, as always – did little to help change matters. There was no opportunity for any sort of education for the majority of the Macedonians, not to mention the higher education. Even the first Yugoslavia between the two world wars tried to stamp out all that was specifically Macedonian. There were very few schools in Macedonia on the secondary level, and there was only a nucleus of the philosophical faculty of Skopje before the war.

A.A.: What is happening now is a deliberately created phenomenon called the Macedonian Literary Renaissance.

ŠUNJIĆ: It concerns both the language and literature. On the one hand the linguists of Macedonia are trying to build up a fit instrument for literature out of the neglected speech of a people that has been illiterate for centuries. One of the principal tasks of that group has been accomplished by the poet and linguist Blaže Koneski, who published a great dictionary of the Macedonian language. A Macedonian grammar is also in existence. At the same time the creative work of contemporary Macedonian artists is laying the foundation of something that might become the basis of a new literary tradition. In other words, we have a new language and new literature.

A.A.: But this creation of a brand new literature for a brand new state breeds special problems, particularly that of relating a new-found industrialization – with all that means of urbanization of standards – with the existing tradition. This theme is taken up by James Leech, an Englishman who lectures at Skopje University:

LEECH: What one feels is that modern Macedonian art is cut off from its roots. If one thinks of what really represents old Macedonia – what I call old Macedonia – one's faced with the fact that Macedonia has a history, a history which includes Alexander the Great, which includes the wars against the Byzantine empire, which includes the persecution, as they call it, under the Turks.

Now that history means to the modern Macedonian almost nothing. It's a cliché. It's a thing they believe in. It's a thing they accept. But it's a thing which doesn't do anything for them. What does something for the modern Macedonian is perhaps their history during the war, their resistance to Germany rather than their resistance to Basil II, their resistance to the difficulties of keeping up with the other republics, perhaps a little of their pre-war history, the treatment they received under Serbia, the feeling that some of them have – perhaps most of them have, if one's honest – that part of their country is still not theirs, that they haven't got the whole of Macedonia, a part of it is still enslaved in some way. That's there, but more for them, as far as history goes, is the idea of the history of what Macedonia will be, and not the history of what Macedonia has been.

You see, it seems to me that the Macedonians are separated from their past first of all, of course, by the five hundred years of Turkish occupation; and now that they are free they're really not free to turn to their past, even if they wanted to. One feels that they can't face their past. You see, they've never been really free to face their past before. First of all, the Byzantines wanted to make them part of the Byzantine empire; then the Turks came and wanted to make them part of the Turkish empire; and then Serbia and Bulgaria in the nineteenth century tried to make them part of their kingdoms; and before the last war, when they finally escaped from Turkey, Serbia again wanted to make them part of Serbia. Now that they are free and they can be themselves, somehow they don't want to make themselves Macedonian either. They want to make themselves into a modern socialist state.

A.A.: What Leech is implying is that the local idiosyncracies and rhythms which can help a literature to its special strengths and distinctions tend to get lost in the more anonymous processes of industrialization. The result is a kind of abstract, theoretical ideal of life:

LEECH: I feel that somehow the Macedonian writer thinks too much about Macedonia and listens too little to Macedonia. The one thing that is most lacking in Macedonian writing is real dialogue. The characters in the Macedonian story or a Macedonian novel talk, but they don't talk as the Macedonians I – with my poor Macedonian – hear talking in the street.

A.A.: It is probable that this technical failing comes, above all, from the failure of a significant literary talent to emerge as yet from Macedonia. It may also be that Leech, as an outsider, rather romanticizes the potential strength of a tradition which is associated, in the minds of those in it, with so much backwardness and repression. In the circumstances, they can't go back, they must go forward.

Yet the situation in Macedonia is a pure and concentrated microcosm of the perennial cultural situation in Yugoslavia as a whole. It is a country which, culturally as well as politically, has always been divided in itself: between the eastern and western Roman empires, the Orthodox and Catholic Churches, the Ottoman and Austro-Hungarian empires. And now it maintains an uneasy neutral balance between Europe's Eastern and Western *blocs*. The effect of this has been an extraordinary difficulty in creating any sense of a continuous cultural tradition. Not only do different areas have different traditions of differing richness and proceeding at different speeds, but also several of them have great gaps in their literature which are scarcely bridged at all.

HRISTIĆ: The main characteristic of Serbian literary and cultural tradition is that the 'film track' – as it were – was cut or broken many, many times. These breakings were not due to purely artistic or literary reasons; instead, it is the wars which provide the most important dates in the history of our literature. You in England speak of the literature between the two world wars, but in speaking of Serbian literature you must be always aware of the fact that there always existed two wars in between which you can put any literary period you choose to speak about.

A.A.: A Croatian literary critic defined it this way:

IVAN KUŠAN: Continuous with breaks. I think with breaks which really always meant the starting of something new.

A.A.: When I spoke to Ivo Andrić the Nobel-Prize-winning Bosnian novelist, he laid the blame for the country's cultural backwardness – or unevenness – squarely on the five hundred years of Turkish occupation. 'It drew,' he said, 'a line across the country cutting it off from Europe.' That line can be traced fairly precisely on a map. The main part of the city of Belgrade ends in the Kalemegdan Park, which is on the promontory jutting out over the confluence of the Danube and the Sava. That is the northernmost tip of the Balkan peninsula proper: beyond is the Pannonian Plain. The Turks never really had much influence beyond this little jut of land. But south of it they remained in power, despite the Serbian uprising in 1804, from the time of the Battle of Kosovo, 1389, until the late nineteenth century. They were not wholly clear of the country until 1912. It was five hundred years of emptiness. Although they converted a fair number to Islam, the Turks had no cultural influence at all on the people whose lands they occupied – except, by their brutality, to cultivate the spirit of rebellion. To the superficial observer the entire legacy of the Ottoman empire is a few mosques and a national taste for sweet black coffee.

The result of this great hole in history is two-fold. First is the extreme backwardness and poverty of a large part of the country. Andrić quoted to me a remark by his distinguished fellow-novelist, Miroslav Krleža: 'We are boring a tunnel,' he said, 'through from the fourteenth century to the present.' And Andrić himself commented dryly on the state of Yugoslav literature: 'First we must have typewriters, then we can worry about what to type.' The second consequence of this Turkish Vacancy is the permanent discontinuity of culture.

LADAN: The Turkish occupation changed the picture of the culture generally and radically. For instance, the Croats were not occupied by Turks, though certain regions of Croatia on the borderlines were also taken by Turks. But the general body of Croatian culture had continued one thousand years from the eleventh century to the twentieth. But if you take Serbia and Bosnia the situation was quite different because there was, as a matter of fact, practically five hundred years of Turkish occupation – a great hole – though during even that period there were certain writings and some writers. But it was more of a religious nature and a kind of educational writing than real literature in a proper sense.

A. A. : Nowadays there seems to be an attempt to create a continuous tradition by resurrecting forgotten or obscure poets.

HRISTIĆ : There were, for instance, some poets who were forgotten for this, that, or another reason, and we are now publishing their selected or collected works, as well as various anthologies and a vast publication called *Serbian Literature in 100 Books*, just to bridge those gaps which existed in the history of our literature. I have in mind two periods which were up to now almost completely neglected both by the historians of literature and the critics, namely the Middle Ages and the eighteenth century. The official, academic opinion was that there is no good poetry in them. But there existed a Serbian literature in the Middle Ages – not just popular, not just folk literature – which has a definite literary value and literary merit. On the other hand, there was a strong eighteenth-century literary tradition in the northern parts of the country – across the river Sava – which was also neglected because of its somewhat artificial classicism and its language: it was half Serbian and half Russian, incapable of any further development. It was a dead, still-born language, but nevertheless some poets succeeded in writing very good poetry in it. But the whole point of digging up the past, to my mind, is not to produce a 'back to the Middle Ages' or a 'back to the eighteenth century' movement – personally I would have little sympathy with either of them – but to make ourselves feel more comfortable: there is not just empty space gaping behind, or nothing but wars.

A.A.: Personally, I doubt if this is much more than a patriotic and scholarly game. This, certainly, is the opinion of one of the most talented young Yugoslav poets, Ivan Lalić:

LALIĆ: It is true that speaking of poetry here one can compile beautiful anthologies to show seven centuries of continuity. But it is also true that the language in which our poetry is written today got its definite outlines just a century or two ago. Of course, it is also possible to try to build a tradition out of discontinuities, putting a stress on them. But I do not believe much in poetry playing Robinson Crusoe, and a Crusoe with total amnesia. Fortunately it's even impossible. The language itself took its shape on a ground crowded with history, a ground filled up with remnants of several millennia which are present if you just want them to be present. I like the idea of Orpheus being a poet from the Balkans – that's what he was, anyway.

A.A.: The Orphean ideal is particularly relevant, since there is one kind of poetry which stretches through Yugoslav culture from its beginning up to the present day: that is, the oral folk epics. It is to these that you are always referred when the question of tradition comes up. No doubt they are a genuine, ancient and fairly vital art form. Two Harvard professors, Lord and Parry, who recorded twelve thousand of these songs and epics, showed that they have links with a tradition going back to Homer. And at some time or other most Yugoslav writers – since the epics were rediscovered at the beginning of the century – have had to come to grips with them. But, however impressive they sometimes are, I can't believe that these folk poems have any dynamic cultural effect.

It is, in fact, typical of the limitations of folk art that the narrative pattern, as well as the myths, *can* be traced back to Homer. For folk art is always a bit reactionary. It doesn't change and develop. It may keep alive certain community traditions or myths; it may even be very beautiful at times. But it is never an evolving, developing art-form. To become that, it must be taken up by a sophisticated artist – as Coleridge took the ballads collected by Bishop Percy and produced, with that impetus, *The Ancient Mariner*. Whereupon it ceases to be folk art. This is more or less what happened in Yugoslavia. The poet Miodrag Pavlović describes this.

PAVLOVIĆ: It was most alive, or at least we had the greatest number of documents, only at the beginning of the nineteenth century. It is purely oral culture. And so when poetic culture in a modern sense started to be alive at the end of the eighteenth century, poets first tried to write according to European models. They began with imitations of European classicism. Then the Romantic movement came, which relied heavily on the folk tradition. This collision between the Romantics, who insisted on the national character of the culture, and the classicists, who were oriented towards Europe, was very bitter.

A.A.: Yet it was out of this clash that the basis of modern Serbian poetry was formed.

LALIĆ: The great reformer of the language Vuk Karadžić started a literature which is the root of the modern literature and modern language today. But it would be wrong to suppose that everything started with him. There was, for instance, a well-developed eighteenth-century literature in Vojvodina, written in a language which was rather artificial. In order to introduce the new language and to lay the foundations for the modern literature Vuk Karadžić was forced to abolish, to destroy that literature which was existing, and written in a different language.

First of all he made the folk epics known to the world. The interest for Yugoslav folk epics starts at that time, and it coincides with the general interest for folk-lore in Europe. That's a rather common Romantic trait, isn't it? The language in which those folk epics had been written is more or less the modern language we speak nowadays. In the name of this language, of these folk epics, Vuk Karadžić abolished a whole literature and put a line under a whole development of the century or more before him. As Vuk Karadžić flourished in the first half of the nineteenth century – he was a friend of the brothers Grimm and he was in correspondence with Goethe – he had to fight a very bitter battle to break through with his ideas. There was a whole set of writers, a whole literature, which was against him but which was, at the same time, historically doomed to disappear. At least, to disappear for a century or so, its principal values re-emerging alive in our days. Vuk Karadžić had also the honour to be the creator of the first phonetic alphabet; every child in a primary school learns about it in the first grade.

A.A. : This is a more-or-less regular development of literature in Eastern Europe. The national literatures emerge with nationalist feelings around the middle of the nineteenth century. However flourishing earlier periods of culture may have been, modern work rarely has roots which reach back beyond the Romantics, and often not so far. Instead of being involved in a continuous national tradition, the writers of small countries tend to create influences, artificially, from the literature of all over Europe. Sveto Petrović, who, as a Croatian critic, has more local work to refer to than his Serbian colleagues, discusses this:

PETROVIĆ : In Croatian literature I think you may distinguish, generally speaking, three periods. One of them in the time of the Renaissance, the second one in the nineteenth century, and the third one in the twentieth. I think Croatian literature of the twentieth century is not a real continuation of the literature of the former times. It has to do more with the European trends of the time than with the Croatian literature of the nineteenth and, say, the sixteenth century.

LALIĆ: Speaking of tradition, one must mention the fact that history has conditioned the various peoples of Yugoslavia to be open and sensitive to what is happening in the world around, to assimilate different values and turn them into elements of new values of their own in order to survive, to last, in order to continue.

A.A.: This openness to the literature of the rest of Europe is more than a sign of cultural taste, it's a necessity. I asked Pavlović if a modern Yugoslav poet could produce highly developed work without knowing the literature of other languages – if, in short, there was enough in the national culture on its own to nourish him artistically. He replied with a flat 'No'. And that, with different reservations and qualifications, was the answer I got from most of the other writers. Ivan Kušan, a short-story writer and art critic, who has recently written a fierce attack on the abstract painters who imitate European styles, admitted it:

KUŠAN: I think there are poets who don't speak any foreign languages. But they come to the essence of a foreign culture through their friends, their colleagues who know it.

A.A.: This necessary cosmopolitanism produces a curious paradox which is obvious on all levels. In Belgrade, for example, the intelligentsia is highly sophisticated, well read, relatively well travelled and startlingly polyglot; most are not merely literate, they are *literary* in at least four or five languages. And they produce a sophisticated, cosmopolitan, *avant-garde* art – including, incidentally, some modern buildings which put to shame most of the stuff which is going up in London now.

Yet the streets of Belgrade are full of leather-faced peasants in felt boots, shawls, skull caps and sheepskin jackets. Granted, there has been a big shift of population into the towns in the last few years; before the war seventy-five per cent of the population was non-urban, now only fifty per cent is. Yet the peasants in Belgrade, too numerous to be casual visitors, seem untouched by town habits and dress. Although it is a large, busy, rowdy city it still has that element of idle curiosity which you rarely find in capitals. At any minor, but unexpected noise in the street, everyone stops to attend: the loungers get off their park benches to peer about, the children stop playing, the old men stop gossiping. If you stop in the street and look up at a high window, in no time at all a crowd has gathered and is craning with you. The reasons for this may be boredom, interest, or credulity, but it is, anyway, a long way from the self-absorbed rush of most city life, and even farther from the sophisticated intensities of Belgrade's own intellectual life.

This split is everywhere; you are aware of it from the moment you arrive. Belgrade airport, for example, is one of the most elegant buildings in Europe. But though it is only a few miles from the centre of the city, it seems to be in the middle of nothing. The road from it takes you without a break from the deepest country straight in to the shining, unfinished skyscraperland of Novi Beograd. It is the same in literature. On one side is primitivism: the centuries-old tradition of those oral folk epics which are still sung in the mountains; the bitter but now successful battle against illiteracy. On the other is the highly cosmopolitan, Europeanized sophistication of the urban writers. Occasionally these two elements come together. In, for example, the prose of the young writer Miodrag Bulatović whose fierce, bristlingly clever symbolic novel about a peasant wedding, *The Red Cockerel*, was published here in 1962. Lalić gives an example of the same kind of fusion in verse:

LALIĆ: The poet Vasko Popa, whom I consider one of the best contemporary poets in Yugoslavia, found his own approach to folk-lore. He didn't try to learn something from the epic poetry, but he felt for his roots in folk

91

incantations, in smaller lyric poems, in something I would call nonsense poetry, which exists in our folk-lore as well as in the English – Good Mother Goose in Serbo-Croat.

A.A.: But the general trend of modern Yugoslav poetry, including Popa's, is towards something much more difficult and abstruse: Pavlović's complex, intellectual variations on Greek myths, Hristić's cool and precise irony, or Lalić's highly skilled technique of sensuous impressionism. Let me give an example of this: his poem called 'Orpheus Singing'.

> He sang with a voice like a bush full of roses,
> With a voice of copper, of fruit, of foam,
> And each branch of each tree stretched out, dissolving
> Its stiff bark to softness, soft as though offering
> Its darkish body to a girl's caresses.
>
> And the marvellous beasts couldn't even tell
> That their blood was congealing in golden honey.
> They stood there rampant, the great and the small,
> Each as though carved out of silence, each
> With a lake of light in its listening ear.
>
> And he made time audible
> Gave it the fluency of clear shallow water
> Where, dun, red and speckled,
> The massed trout flicker;
> He gave it the taste of crisp, sunny earth.
>
> He sang on and on as the warm rain fell,
> Standing there drenched in the violet clover,
> While under his smooth skin his blood raced to catch
> The echo of his ripe voice in the rocks,
> There where the first wave of silence broke.

That kind of extreme sensuality combined with extreme technical sophistication has more obvious roots in, say, French poetry than in anything that is readily apparent in Yugoslavia.

There is much the same dichotomy in the visual arts. On one side are the cosmopolitan and highly skilled abstractions of a painter like Miodrag Protić, director of Belgrade's National Gallery and winner of several international prizes, or the very personal surrealism of Maljenko Stančić; on the other are the deliberate and, to my mind, rather mannered simplicities of the school of modern primitives, the best known of whom is Ivan Generalić. Again they come together in the one Yugoslav artist who is certainly in the international class and has a large international reputation, the sculptor Ivan Meštrović, who died in 1962. But in general the arts tend to polarize around extremes.

These paradoxes have recently come in for a good deal of discussion. In his New Year speech Marshal Tito attacked the abstract painters and said that the state would no longer buy their work. Now, part of this attack coincided with the new burst of amiability between Belgrade and Moscow. And these things are normally conducted like Salome's dance: each side shows its good faith by a mutual exchange of heads on platters. Last time, the heads were those of Molotov and Djilas. This time it seems to be the abstract painters who are under the axe. But it's also certain that Tito's statement was a good deal more restrained and circumspect than Khrushchev's outburst of bull-headed philistinism at about the same time. Tito linked his criticisms with an attack on *kitsch* culture – the craze for imported gangster stories and souped-up versions of the classics – which means it can be interpreted as an attack less on abstract art as such, than on second-rate imitations and fashion-mongering.

That, anyway, was the interpretation hopefully adopted by most of the communist intellectuals I discussed the problem with.

PETROVIĆ: Immediately after the war until the fifties, the only art that was exhibited – I mean paintings and sculpture – was of so-called socialistic realism. But after '52, the influence of Western art, even of Western abstract art, through the more frequent contacts with the West, grew stronger and stronger. The situation a year ago was that all the art was dominated in Yugoslavia by the group of abstract artists. Only their works were to be purchased by the state, you know, and that was a very serious thing. That's why Tito spoke.

LADAN: I would never say that Tito said the same things as Khrushchev. There is a great difference. Tito was only talking about a kind of a flood on the market of bad art, a flood of cheap things, but Khrushchev was taking quite a basic line on the whole style and culture. As for the arts, only the connoisseurs of art should give judgements on it, should say what's good and what's bad. But there can be also the general reaction against the overflood of very cheap stuff on the general market.

KUŠAN: I think it would be very bad to discourage *avant-garde* art, any form of it. But the situation was not very sympathetic when *avant-garde* art almost became the only style which was encouraged, when it was almost identified with the state art, with the ideal of art. I think some of the apologists for art in our country would say that it is the normal art which belongs to the *avant-garde* social class or *avant-garde* political movement.

A.A.: Granted the usual element of deviousness in this kind of discussion, what is interesting is the way in which it gets back continually to the problem of creating a specifically Yugoslavian image – an image which will owe as little as possible to either the East or the West. It was, after all, this independence which got Yugoslavia into its present curious neutrality. The Partisan army drew its moral strength from a centuries-old tradition: that of savage resentment of the occupiers. And the fact that Tito was already in control of a large part of the country when the war ended meant that the Yugoslavs were by no means wholly dependent on the Russians for their liberation.

Independence is, in fact, a main element in that most discussed of all subjects in Yugoslavia: the *slovenska dusa*, the slavic soul. As for its other elements, they could probably be arranged into neat enough pairs of opposites: fanaticism and cynicism, mysticism and irresponsibility, melodrama and knowingness, anarchism, and a passion for causes, great feeling and an equally great flair for boredom, super-cultivation and deep ignorance. As Andrić remarked, there is a permanent crisis of the soul in the country.

To find the artistic means to express these contradictions, the Yugoslavs are willing to use whatever suits their purposes from whatever foreign cultures seem convenient. Krleža's novel *The Return of Philip Latinovic*, for example, begins with a Thomas Mann-like analysis of exhausted gloom and decadence, and ends in pure Dostoevskian excesses. But perhaps the country's most distinguished novelist is also the most significant: Ivo Andrić. He is not typical, in that his work has nothing to do with modern experimentation. Essentially he is a nineteenth-century novelist, very historically minded and writing in a cool, deliberate, detailed style, rather like a pessimistic, guilt-ridden Stendhal. But I feel that he is building up in his two great long novels – *The Bridge Over the Drina* and *Bosnian Story* – not just a history of Yugoslavia but also a Yugoslav way of looking at history. *Bosnian Story*, for example, is Tolstoy's *War and Peace* retold from the periphery of European civilization. It has as its background the same events – the rise and fall of Napoleon – but they echo only very faintly on that far edge of Europe where they are scarcely noticeable. They are echoed in the sensibility of a cultured, depressed French diplomat who is exiled in the alien, intensely hostile Oriental community of Travink. He is beaten and emptied by the place, until his own will becomes as frozen and hopeless as the landscape. Perhaps the most crucial speech in the whole book is that made by a Levantine doctor:

It is the lot of Levantines to be *poussière humaine*, human dust, drifting drearily between East and West, belonging to neither and pulverized by both. . . . They are victims of the fatal division of mankind into Christian and non-Christian, eternal interpreters and go-betweens, who nevertheless carry within themselves so much that is unclear and inarticulate. . . . They are a little sub-section of humanity, staggering under a double load of original sin: they need saving and redeeming a second time, but no one can see how or through whom it can be done. They are frontier folk, spiritually and physically, from those bleak and bloody lines of division which through some terrible, absurd misunderstanding have been drawn between man and man, God's creatures between whom there should not and must not be any such division.

In the novel the speaker is a Levantine – a member of a tiny minority group within an already tiny nation. But he might equally be describing, analysing and apologizing for the perennial conflict in the *slovenska dusa*, as it vacillates between gloom and energy. But nowadays the redemption he speaks of will presumably be political – if it ever comes.

Part II: U.S.A.

(January and February 1964)

5. Kennedy and the Intellectuals

THE first warning I got was in the plane, as we approached New York. 'This is John F. Kennedy,' said a soothing voice on the intercom. 'Please fasten your seat belts and refrain from smoking.' My instinctive reaction was: We are flying too high. Admittedly, I'd been dozing and had woken in a panic, but none of the other explanations seemed feasible: a terrible coincidence with the pilot's name? A sick joke? A happening? It took me some moments to work out that what had been announced was Idlewild by its new name. It swallowed us all up, gleaming, warm and sound-proofed; even the Customs men were friendly. Yet that sense of being put off-centre in a macabre way – a sense of the absurd – seemed to pervade everything and everybody.

On the surface, nothing much had changed. The New York pace was still as murderous as the drinking habits. The new buildings still rose as plentifully and brilliantly as the flowers in spring. The *New York Times* still carried the same picture of Jimmy Hoffa over the same megalomaniac pronouncements by him as it had when I left three years before. Yet despite all the same old hectoring, bustling, back-biting, party-going energy, there seemed, among the intellectuals, a curious lack of conviction, something between enervation and nervousness. This rudderless depression is, I think, a direct consequence of the assassination of President Kennedy. Norman Mailer, one of America's most important novelists, describes this feeling:

MAILER: We'd gotten into a curious kind of complacency during the Kennedy years, because all sorts of rather interesting, gossipy things were happening all over the place, yet nothing was happening, no violence was erupting. What I mean is, no personal individual violence was erupting. Certainly large violent social phenomena were taking place. But they had to take place. We'd known for years that they would take place sooner or later – for instance the war of the Negroes and the whites – but when this particular act of personal violence, the assassination, took place, it threw us all back badly. If the nature of American life was much more violent than we thought it was, then the alternatives became gloomier. Either one had to accept a further totalitarization of American life – more security everywhere – or one had to recognize the fact that our life had become simply more dangerous than it used to be. The air in America since Kennedy's death – at least in intellectual circles – has been close to that of a continuing wake. I can never remember so many of us being so depressed in a flat way for so long about the possibilities of things.

A.A.: But why did the intellectuals take it harder than anyone else? Of course, the whole population – with the exception of a few ignorant madmen in the South – was shocked and grieving. Yet, paradoxically, it was the intellectuals who seemed most appalled by the outrage in Dallas. I say 'paradoxically' because I suspect that had the victim been another president – Eisenhower, Truman, even Johnson – the intellectuals would have taken it more coolly, certainly less personally. Their intense involvement with Kennedy and his assassination had, I think, three main causes: first, there was the man himself and what he represented; second, there was what he'd done for the humanities and arts, and the new status he'd given them; third, there was his murder itself and what it manifested of the under-forces in American life.

First, then, Kennedy the man. Norman Podhoretz, literary critic and Editor of *Commentary*, begins:

PODHORETZ: Kennedy's style was superb. He was a man of enormous charm, wit, cleverness. If you got up close to him it was quite impossible to resist him. He handled himself very beautifully at Press Conferences, though I think his formal speeches were far more conventional than most people seemed to think they were. Nevertheless, it's difficult to know exactly what the general public attitude was. That is, Kennedy was a glamorous figure to the American public, but his youth, his wealth, his beautiful wife, his almost kind of fairy-tale existence and career had, I think, more to do with this in the public mind than anything that you might call intellectuality.

A.A.: Murray Kempton, one-time political columnist of the *New York Post* and now Editor of the *New Republic*, isolates a significant element of this glamour:

KEMPTON: Kennedy had been shot at in the war and had conducted himself magnificently. There's always a question with a lot of us as to whether we really have physical courage. I don't think this was ever too much of a problem with Kennedy. He had gone through the war and had been a combat soldier, and the matter of his masculinity, of his toughness, was solved for him.

A.A.: This courage of Kennedy's had great imaginative appeal, as the poet, Robert Lowell, explains:

LOWELL: We have some sort of faith, that the man who can draw most quickly is the real hero. He's proved himself. Yet that's a terribly artificial standard; the real hero might be someone who'd never get his pistol out of the holster and who'd be stumbling about and near-sighted and so forth. But we don't want to admit that. It's deep in us that the man who draws first somehow has proved himself. Kennedy represents a side of America that's appealing to the artist in retrospect, a certain heroism. And you feel, in certain terms, he really was a martyr in his death. He was reckless, went further than the office called for; perhaps you'd say that he was fated to be killed. And that's an image one could treasure and it stirs one.

A.A.: After the eight-year reign of Big Daddy Eisenhower, America was ripe for a hero. This was the great attraction of the man. Yet it wasn't his heroism that affected the intellectual tone of the country so much. It was the other qualities which went with the toughness, which the toughness, as it were, justified in the eyes of the general public. In the White House, I talked to Arthur Schlesinger Jr, a close personal friend of the late President and a member of his Brains Trust:

SCHLESINGER: The thing about Kennedy was that he enjoyed the world of ideas. He wasn't precisely an intellectual – I suppose very few people in politics in the contemporary world are – but he liked the company of intellectuals, he was not intimidated by them, he delighted in conversation about ideas and history and the theatre and the arts. More than that, in a certain sense, he made the whole role of an intellectual acceptable. Kennedy himself was a war hero, a tough naval politician, a young man who, in any hard and rough world, could more than hold his own. In this respect, there is a difference perhaps between Kennedy and Stevenson: because Kennedy and Stevenson had much the same attitude towards these things, but Kennedy was a more Roman type and, one might say, Stevenson a more Greek type. It was Kennedy's espousal of this cause, so to speak, which probably commanded a larger acceptance for the role of the intellectual than might otherwise be possible.

A.A.: For some, this intellectual tone was something quite new in American politics.

PODHORETZ: Kennedy as a symbolic figure represented, I suppose unconsciously for most people, consciously for some, the first major public figure who was genuinely of our time. One felt him to be a contemporary. He was a man who was post-Freud, post-Marx, post-Einstein; he was a man who lived in the twentieth century. What I mean is that there is no such person as the public figure that most American politicians pretend to be. This is a mythological personage who is based on all kinds of nineteenth-century ideas, small-town, rural – Lyndon Johnson, for example, seems to be projecting that kind of image. Kennedy was clearly a twentieth-century, sophisticated, urban man.

SCHLESINGER: America is a pluralist society and it's hard to say that Eisenhower is more American than Kennedy or that Hoover was more American than Roosevelt. Both represent deep strains of American life. I think that Kennedy and Roosevelt in a certain sense do represent a patrician, eastern-seaboard, Ivy League culture, but that's an authentic part of American life. In Kennedy, as in Roosevelt, you had a certain cosmopolitan urbanity which produced an invariable courtesy and grace in personal relationships, in public style, and so on. Indeed, the whole revival of the word 'style' is itself an expression of the impact of Kennedy. It has now become odious in its overuse, but it is symptomatic of the impact that Kennedy made. It can be said, I think, that Kennedy was probably the most civilized man to sit in the White House since Jefferson.

A.A.: The force of his civilized style was unquestionable and, in a sense, two-edged. It not only changed the attitude of the general public towards the intellectuals, it also changed the attitude of the intellectuals towards politicians. In the States, the gap between the two is even greater than it is in England. It had seemed peculiarly unbridgeable after the long sleep of Eisenhower's régime, with its McCarthy inquisition and government by big business men. Kennedy changed all this utterly, as Hannah Arendt, the political philosopher and one of the most original thinkers in America, pointed out:

ARENDT: He represented actually a different concept of

103

politics. Even those who play the political game in this country usually don't have a very high opinion of what they're doing, whereas Kennedy had the highest possible opinion of what he was doing. Perhaps he exaggerated, but that is a fact. And he really gave this whole realm a kind of dignity and intellectual splendour – whatever you may call it – which it never had before, even under Roosevelt. I do not want to give any impression that this was an intellectual or a very highly motivated idealist and so on. This was really somebody whose whole life was determined by a sense for action. And that is so extremely rare – that is, on a high level – so extremely rare in our century, that when it comes nobody knows what to do with it.

A.A.: The question is, then, how did Kennedy's political genius for action join up with his much less professional taste for the arts and humanities? The man most involved in the official, governmental encouragement of the arts was August Heckscher, whom Kennedy invited to the White House as his Special Consultant on the arts:

HECKSCHER: One of the surprising things which President Kennedy did – surprising certainly in its results and its impact – was the simple act of inviting a hundred and fifty or so intellectuals and scholars and artists to his Inauguration back in January 1961. That simple deed was an affirmation that the intellectual doesn't stand any more at the fringe of the national life, an odd and perhaps a dangerous person, but is one of the crucial figures in the whole democratic community.

After the Inauguration, it seemed necessary and prudent to the President that he should do something which would mean that the impetus of that great day should not be lost and that all this promise should not prove vain. I think he searched about for a good while as to how he could give some form of implementation to these impulses, to this new interest which had been aroused by the Inauguration and also by some of the things that Mrs Kennedy was doing in the White House – the dinners she held for musicians and artists and poets and so on. This all came to a head when President Kennedy invited me to come down and establish a modest experimental office in the White House to see what we could do to ensure a more fruitful relationship between government and the arts. The President originally said: 'Come down and look about at what is going on in America and see those points at which government can be helpful within the policies that are practical and feasible; and those points where perhaps government today is inadvertently impeding the arts or placing burdens, unfair burdens, upon the artist and the intellectual – as in policies of taxation and things of that sort.'

So I went down to the White House and I looked about as he had urged me to do. I saw him from time to time in the day's work, as we discussed practical matters which did come up. And I came to feel, before my time there was over, that there's an enormous amount which can be done by the right individual rightly placed in intervening in the innumerable government decisions which are made every day to see that the cause of good taste, good design, the cause of the arts, is represented.

We were always getting cases brought to me in that little White House office: the Highway Department was about to put a road through a liberal arts college that was part of our cultural heritage; the Post Office Department was about to tear down a very good old building and construct a very bad new one in its place; and so on. Kennedy was wonderful at creating an atmosphere where the community of the arts felt that he had access to them and that they had access to him. But the main thing, of course, is to have a President who does read books, who even occasionally writes books, who is naturally sympathetic to the men of intellect and spirit in the community. And that President Kennedy certainly was and did.

PODHORETZ: The main thing that Kennedy did was to

give intellectuals a sense of connexion to power. This was quite unprecedented in the experience of most of us. One heard that he read the magazines one wrote for. He seemed to know most of our names. He seemed to be interested, often in a gossipy sort of way, in what was being said around town. And I don't know exactly what effect this kind of thing had, but it certainly did for the first time make you feel that Washington was not a bottomless well of inattention. I suspect, incidentally, that that sense of reassurance that a lot of us had the first year largely of the Kennedy administration was probably an illusion. That is, I'm not sure that it was anything more than a symbolic change. I'm not sure that the Kennedy administration was especially receptive to the ideas of the American intellectual world. It was interested in them, but I don't know that it did anything in direct response to them.

A.A.: The literary critic and Editor of the *Partisan Review*, Philip Rahv, put it more strongly:

RAHV: Kennedy didn't really have any idea what went on in the intellectual world. The Kennedy thing was more social, it was sophisticated. Kennedy was not so much an intellectual as a sophisticated person – a product of Boston and Harvard. He knew a great many intellectuals, he understood to some extent how to value them and how to estimate their contribution. But what he did about intellectuals had no consequence as far as the basic features of American intellectual life and the alienation of intellects from politics are concerned. There are people who imagine that if a President invites them to dinner the pattern of American society has changed. But it has not in the least degree changed. There is a big gap between the brain-washing mass media conduct so far as the mind of the basic population is concerned, and the mind of the intellectual minority, which can't be bridged by these social menus of the Kennedys. I don't believe that he thought it could be.

A.A.: Elizabeth Hardwick, one of the editors of the brilliant new fortnightly magazine, the *New York Review of Books*, takes this up from a different angle:

HARDWICK: What's happened here that made Kennedy seem rather sweeter than he would have otherwise to people, is this sense that there's no real *avant-garde*. To find a president who at least keeps up with what is chic, alas, connects him with the intelligentsia in some funny way. If there were a real *avant-garde*, they would feel that they had something that could be kept apart from the chicness. But it's all the same thing. Everybody is famous – all the writers, no matter what you do. It's rather hard to avoid being acceptable, and the Kennedys had a real regard for what you'd call interesting people. But that's not the same as being one of us, as intellectuals would sometimes say. Yet it's as close as anyone's come. But you can't imagine, even in the thirties, that any large group of people would have felt that that kind of person was particularly interested in their future.

A.A.: In a sense, then, Kennedy, with his impeccable sense of style, used the intellectuals as window-dressing, to add cultural tone to his administration.

ARENDT: They were drawn into it, either as members of the Brains Trust – I think he pretty much emptied the Harvard faculty – or as guests of the White House. And of the two I think the latter was in some way, after the style of the man, much more important than the former. I'm not so sure to what an extent he listened, or would have listened or gone on listening to the advice given by the gentlemen from Harvard, but I'm pretty sure he would have gone on under all circumstances with those curious dinner invitations which were extended to the whole intellectual community all over the country.

A.A.: What, then, were these curious dinners like, which

were so much discussed and had such odd reverberations on the American scene?

LOWELL: I think of Edmund Wilson's comment. Arthur Schlesinger was asking him how he felt about being invited to the White House to dinner and Edmund said: 'Oh, it was bigger than other dinners.'

I was invited there for Malraux's dinner, and Kennedy made a rather graceful joke that 'the White House was becoming almost a café for intellectuals . . .'. We all drank a great deal, and had to sort of be told not to take our champagne into the concert, to put our cigarettes out – like children – though nicely; it wasn't peremptory. Then the next morning you read that the Seventh Fleet had been sent somewhere in Asia and you had a funny feeling of how unimportant the artist really was: that this was sort of window-dressing and the real government was somewhere else, and that something much closer to the Pentagon was really ruling the country.

A.A.: But if these glittering dinner parties were rather to one side of the real business of governing, they served at least two purposes: they advanced the general status of the intellectuals in the community, and they also gave Kennedy some sense of what currents were actually running in the country below the complex political eddies which were his main concern.

MAILER: It wasn't only that the intellectuals had status, but we became just a touch like minor royalty. Dispossessed of our natural lands, squatting in other people's palaces, there was always Versailles. One could be called to Washington. For some the call came, for others the call never came. And Kennedy did very much act like a king *vis-à-vis* the intellectuals. He had any number of couriers who would pass his messages, you see. They would say in effect 'Jack sends his love', something of the sort kings and consummate politicans do all the time, because it costs them absolutely nothing. The message is given in great secret and doesn't even have to be denied. I mean you wouldn't go round and repeat it.

But I think that one of the marvellous things about Kennedy was that he did have a sense of how delicate and unpredictable and useful the intellectual Establishment could be to him. And I think it was quite sincere; I think he wanted the intellectual Establishment to be part of America. But he also had this exquisite politician's sense of how it could be used, which no other President I think had ever had. He knew that in some funny way the development of the American novel had some extended tenuous connexions with the more serious central power plays that were going on all the time. What they were, of course . . . well, my guess is, had I been fortunate enough to hear Kennedy talk about it, that he probably had a most marvellous sociologist's view of what public opinion is. In America one of the mysteries that's always intrigued me and I've never been able to solve quite to my own satisfaction, is that we do have a curious kind of influence. It's as if the literary world is like an idler gear between enormous gears. Once in a great while, this idler gear is brought into play and the larger gears turn a tiny bit in relation to us.

A.A.: Now I suspect that the idler gear came into play in the most dramatic and disastrous manner possible on 22 November, 1963. That is, when whatever it was that Kennedy might have learned from the writers caught up with him in Dallas. I will come back to this. But first, what were the immediate effects of Kennedy's intellectual sophistication?

ARENDT: One thing is beyond doubt: the new status of the intellectuals. Professors, for instance, today are somebodies and not nobodies; and this is entirely new and it dates really only a few years. And as everything in this country goes very quick, today the professor in America is almost as highly regarded as he was in European countries, let's say, ten or twenty years ago. Something has changed, and don't forget it coincides with the moment when these intellectuals are really needed. I don't mean the scientists and experts, nor even the teachers and professors. The increase of leisure time in mass society has created a very real need for novelists, critics, editors, artists, etc., all of whom play their part in the entertainment industry.

PODHORETZ: What's happened in this country since about 1948 is what you might describe as an almost complete mobilization of the nation's intellectual resources behind the Cold War. I'm not only thinking of the founding of research institutes like Rand and the Hudson Institute, working on government contracts – you know, specifically on defence problems – but also the fact that almost every major university set up research programmes that were directly connected with foreign-policy aims. Almost every writer, professor, scientist, thinker has been involved in conferences, in State Department-sponsored confabs and trips, and in general there has been a climate created in which the critical function of the intellectual has been suppressed. I don't mean in any conspiratorial way. I mean that it's quite natural, you know – because the money was coming from there – that a relatively uncritical climate, except from a technical point of view, should have been created.

What's very much needed now, and I think may even begin to happen under the Johnson administration, is not just a reconversion of American industry from armaments to peace-time production, but a demobilization of the intellectual and academic communities. Kennedy, incidentally, had a strong sense of this need, though he never did anything about it. He continually stressed, in informal remarks particularly, his interest in divorcing culture from the Cold War. He did make it clear that he knew that cultural life was something that had to be pursued for its own sake, and that a certain corruption had seeped in as a result of the willingness of Washington to give power to intellectuals. This started, of course, long before Kennedy.

A.A.: This new acceptance and establishment bothered the intellectuals even more than it did Kennedy. Nearly all of them regard their alienation as a mark of distinction, a sign of their artistic identity. Lionel Trilling, the literary critic, describes the anxiety that was felt when it began to slip away from them.

TRILLING: In a curious way Kennedy thickened things up and gave people – gave me at any rate, and I think a good many of my friends – a certain sense of our actuality in the social structure. The intellectual seemed to become more important. I'm not sure that the greater importance of the intellectual wasn't something I got worried about. I got a little worried about that easier possibility of the intellectual to move into an established class. When you think of yourself as a literary intellectual, which always implies a certain strongly critical function, the easier acceptance of one in that role in the Kennedy administration seemed to me to be something that one ought to be a little leery of.

A.A.: To some extent the feeling that alienation is a quality to be nursed like a delicate child is part of the American intellectual tradition. Witness, the historian, Richard Hofstadter, who has recently published an excellent book on *Anti-Intellectualism in American Life*.

HOFSTADTER: I think there's something historical and traditional that adds a dimension to this commitment to alienation: it stems from the fact that almost no really important intellectual class in America since the days of the Puritan ministry has been very much at home in this country. Even the genteel, established intellectuals of the mid nineteenth century were in effect patrician rebels against the increasing industrialization and the philistinism of the country. So that it has been the tradition of American intellectuals of all kinds and stamps to find themselves at odds with American society: this, I think, to a degree that is unusual elsewhere.

It seems to me that one of the interesting things about the American intellectual's situation is that, while most of us may think of alienation as a fact of life, he's made something more out of it. He has made alienation into a kind of creed or imperative for himself. And this becomes quite a psychic burden in periods like the present when the intellectual is doing well. We were raised in the twenties and thirties on the assumption that the intellectual had to be at pretty sharp odds with society either for cultural reasons, which were uppermost in the twenties, or for political reasons, which impressed themselves on us in the thirties. We have now arrived at a period in which the intellectual, in one capacity or another, is getting an extraordinary amount of recognition. This is by no means to say that anti-intellectualism has disappeared, but if it has remained prominent it's only because of the intellectual's own salience. Even academics are getting well paid in the United States now. And we haven't got the internal apparatus to absorb this without feeling extraordinarily guilty and edgy about it. I think there is something valuable in the intellectual's alienation. David Riesman once said that he thought that American intellectuals did best for their country when they were most against it. And I think there's a lot to that. But I don't think that alienation can be taken out of the descriptive realm as an account of what happens to sensitive people in modern, mass, mechanized society, and made into a moral imperative. This is what I think American intellectuals are suffering from to a great degree today.

A.A.: To some extent the alienation of the intellectuals is the result of what Robert Lowell calls the 'sheerness' of American society, and their new acceptance is due to the iron powers of digestion of the public-relations machinery. But that is a question for later chapters. The point now is the particular influence of Kennedy's encouragement of the intellectuals on all levels. In one sense he was compensating them for the immediate political past. The highly technological world war which was waged in the forties and the equally technological peace which followed had forced the intellectuals into unusual prominence.

HOFSTADTER: The greater saliency of the intellectual in American life has also resulted in his becoming a more conspicuous target. A perfect illustration of this saliency, of course, is the whole anti-intellectual animus of the McCarthy movement. McCarthy had a lot of targets; intellectuals were only one among them, but they were prominent. And it was clear from the way in which McCarthy's followers crawled out of the woodwork in various localities, persecuting librarians, teachers, professors, and what not, that he aroused a good deal of enthusiasm with this kind of assault. On the other hand, they were being assaulted because they were thought of now as being important enough to be objects of attention. Of course, it's very hard to appreciate that particular kind of recognition.

Another thing that made us very sensitive in the early and middle 1950s was, of course, the political fate of Adlai Stevenson, who was the hero of an overwhelming majority of American intellectuals and whose rejection by the electorate in favour of what we thought was a relatively philistine kind of expression, sensibility and mind, was a repudiation of intellectuals themselves.

A.A.: Kennedy changed all this. He gave greater recognition to the back-room experts in government; he brought into the White House his brilliant Brains Trust of professors – men like Schlesinger and Galbraith – and he lent the enormous prestige of his office to the personal encouragement of the arts and humanities. The problem is to know to what extent the new glamorous status of the intellectual corrupts him from his true function.

HOFSTADTER: His specializing function in that sense tends to create a kind of professional deformation in him. The intellectual is desperately needed as an expert. This has two effects: it creates a kind of quite justified general resentment of expertise – the thing that runs our life – and the whole intellectual class suffers from that resentment, including those who were not in any operative sense here intellectuals. But there is also the more direct effect on him, that it tends to put him in demand for his specialized skills rather than for his general speculative and critical functions. It also creates an environment for him which is in many ways glossy and efficient and glamorous and mechanically intriguing, but which is cold and uniform and overbearing. And we all suffer from this. Intellectuals are more sensitive to it than others, I suppose.

A.A.: The literary critic, Irving Howe, takes this up:

HOWE: If, say, twenty-five or thirty-five years ago the problem of the intellectual was that he was cut out, that he was left out of the society, that he felt himself – as we used to say – 'alienated', today the problem of the intellectual is in a certain sense that he's too much in the society, he's too assimilated to the society. He's overwhelmed with possibilities for making a dollar, for doing jobs. There's an enormous amount of busy work. You can spend your whole life being busy doing all kinds of little chores. It's not a matter of selling out or anything melodramatic like that. It's just that you end up not doing the work for which you have presumably devoted your life. And so you can – and I know plenty of people who have this feeling – you can look back and feel that it's been a whole series of preparations, involvements, but you never got to the main thing. It's in this way that contemporary American life seems to me very dangerous for the intellectual; it sucks him in and absorbs him, it makes him feel too much at home, too much at ease, and he has to learn to keep a certain protective distance from it.

ARENDT: The problem of affluence is, of course, very real – especially in America. The temptations are enormously great, and it is very difficult to withstand them because it's really big money that all of a sudden comes to a class which is not used to that kind of money. I personally think that real poverty and this kind of affluence are about equally bad for intellectuals. What they need is a reasonable amount of security. They should not be really poor and they should not be really rich, because both are distracting.

To the extent that they have become a class, they have, of course, also become philistines. I don't mean all of them. Of course not. But in so far as they are nothing but intellectuals, they are philistines. What else could they possibly be? They are just, as everybody else, members of society and they behave accordingly.

A.A.: The adjustment to wealth, of course, had never been Kennedy's problem. Yet the feeling that Kennedy was with the intellectuals yet separate, that he sympathized with their interests yet was not subject to their temptations – whatever other temptations he *was* subject to – meant that they were tied to him in a curiously close and personal knot. Sometimes the very closeness was the cause of infinite irritation.

PODHORETZ: There was this kind of love–hate relation between Kennedy and the intellectuals, at least those of my kind of circle. He was criticized very, very severely and largely because one took his claims and pretensions so seriously – in a way that one would not ordinarily take the claims and pretensions of a politician. And it was clear from his programmes that many of these pretensions were precisely pretensions and that there was no real driving force or serious energy, political energy, behind these stated aims that many of us found attractive. But you know, one felt – I felt very strongly for example – that a great deal of pressure from the left (and I use that term in a very broad sense) was necessary to neutralize the pressures from the right that were coming at Kennedy at the time. His weakness as President was that he did tend to respond to public pressure and he made very little effort to lead public opinion.

A.A.: Certainly, this kind of criticism was to some extent justified. Kennedy's New Frontier all too often seemed to bog down depressingly close to home – in Congress, to be exact. Equally, his personal charm and apparent interest in cultural matters promoted in the intellectuals a warmth which wasn't quite relevant. That is, they were inclined to feel him to be so much one of them that they were unable to see that his peculiar political power came from his detachment and his skill in using contrasting forces for his own ends. Murray Kempton sums this up cogently:

KEMPTON: The quality Mr Kennedy had which, for example, President Eisenhower didn't have and certainly Mr Johnson doesn't have now, was the feeling that – well, you do have a feeling when you sit and look at the White House that that's *theirs* and there's something that's *ours*. It's a kind of class focal proposition. Mr Kennedy always seemed to me to be *neither's*. And it was a nice feeling that you had really, that you weren't working for him.

MAILER: Kennedy was not only a great man, but he was also a consummate politician, a very coldblooded, even ruthless politician. The result was that as a coldblooded, ruthless politician, he knew enough to know he could not command all phenomena, he knew that he had to lay himself open to all sorts of very interesting criticism. For the first time in our literary life it was possible not only to attack the President, you see, but to attack him as a younger brother, attack with the intensity of a family quarrel. That offered exciting possibilities for a good many of us.

A.A.: I think that the dialectic which went on between Kennedy and the intellectuals was fruitful because the President was a creature of an utterly different kind from that which the intellectuals usually engaged with. For example, the shift from alienation to status, from the role of jester to that of priest, induced in most of them, as we have seen, a profound unease. Perhaps this was an anxiety native only to New York. It was, nevertheless, palpably present. Yet nothing could have been less true of Kennedy himself.

SCHLESINGER: There's always been a difference between New York and Washington. In the time of Roosevelt, for example, the New York intellectuals were extremely suspicious of Roosevelt, hostile to his administration; it's only in retrospect that Roosevelt became a hero to the New York intellectuals. I think partly it has to do with attitudes towards power. I think that the intellectuals in Washington are not made guilty by the exercise of power. Someone like Kennedy, for example, saw power as an opportunity and a responsibility and not something which required a great inner torment or questioning or, as they say, which induced any sense of guilt.

A.A.: Kennedy's intellectuality, in short, was non-idealistic, and non-theoretical. He was, instead, in the American tradition of essentially pragmatic rationalism.

SCHLESINGER: When I said that Kennedy was a man of reason, I did not, however, mean to imply that he was a rationalist. I don't think that he had a classical faith in the serenity or order or rationality of society. He was a man of reason in the sense that William James was a man of reason. You remember James's distinction between the tender-minded and the tough-minded? The tender-minded were monists who saw the universe as an ultimate harmony in which all the parts were related to all the other parts. But the tough-minded in James's sense were those who saw the universe not as one but as many, who believed that there was an intractability about it, who believed that there were genuine issues which could not be reconciled and harmonized, who thought there was a basic discord in the universe. Kennedy was very much on the tough-minded pattern; he was, in James's terms, what one would call a radical empiricist. So that, while he was a man of reason in the way he reached conclusions about public policy, he did not, I think, pre-suppose that order was the basic framework of existence.

A.A.: Radical empiricism is – perhaps by necessity – a habit of mind rooted in the American scene. Even before William James, de Tocqueville had written of the States that:

> Men are no longer bound together by ideas, but by interests; and it would seem as if human opinions were reduced to a sort of intellectual dust, scattered on every side, unable to collect, unable to cohere.

Now, a hundred and thirty years later, the world of ideas and the world of opinions, the world of the intellect and that of psychopathology have drifted farther and more bewilderingly apart. So much so, indeed, that even the most tough-minded radical empiricist would find the abyss between them impossible to bridge.

HOWE: The great danger, I think, is this: that there is more and more dissociation between intellect and social power; I mean social power from the depths. More and more intellectuals think of themselves as relating to Washington, their idea of social power becomes more and more manipulative, regulatory. But less and less do they think of connecting themselves with – if I may use an old-fashioned vocabulary – with the masses, with those who are below. As a consequence of this, those who are below – the oppressed, the minority groups – tend to be inchoate, tend to be inarticulate, and thereby potentially all the more violent.

A.A.: Now it may be that Kennedy for all his wonderful politician's instinct and his practical shrewdness, misjudged this violent underlayer in American life. His civilized grace and wit and charm, his sophistication and cultural ease – in short, all the qualities which made him irresistibly seductive both to the American intellectuals and, as the reaction to his death showed, to all Western Europe – alienated him from the more unpredictable forces of the country.

KEMPTON: I used to sort of complain, you know, that Kennedy overvalued what was eastern and fashionable, and that the real history of the United States was made by completely unexpected people. The best example of this, of course, were the Negro kids in those segregated Negro schools who went and sat down at a lunch counter and got themselves in gaol. They altered the Democratic platform by this particular act, and then went on really to alter the whole climate of discussion. So that you had a period of ten years of conferences of one kind or another by comfortable and respectable people, and then you had one year of these direct-action demonstrations, followed by a kind of engagement with the problem. And this proved to me that Kennedy just did not understand where ideas came from. They came from unknown strangers. Then, of course, Mr Kennedy goes down to Dallas and gets shot by some unknown stranger. And I suddenly realized that all this disorder – which I had not thought about as violence quite so much, just as disorder – produced this kind of thing. I mean you have to face the fact that assassination's a democratic act, and that out of the same particular process which will, for example, produce a novelist like William Faulkner who comes out of whatever unexpected source on the American map, this will also produce whoever it was who assassinated Kennedy.

A.A.: 'Assassination is a democratic act': this, I think, is one of the central and most appalling paradoxes that thinking people in the United States have had to face since Kennedy's death.

KEMPTON: This idea of violence and the acceptance of violence is somehow the acceptance, I think, of the individual's right to complain about society. An American really feels that he is entitled to judge all sorts of opinions and to put them forward as serious opinions about insoluble problems.

I happen to be innocent enough to believe that if the Dallas police force had known that Jack Ruby was a homicidal maniac – and I suppose a man who kills a stranger may be considered a homicidal maniac: if the word, you know, is not pejorative – if they'd known this, they wouldn't have allowed him to hang around. But the point of the matter is they thought he was a strip-tease proprietor, with whom they have a naturally closer relationship than they would with a respectable citizen, and that he was a man like themselves – which means that he wouldn't indulge in an act of violence except for money or under orders from his superior. The appearance of Jack Ruby and the reality were quite a good deal different. And we do happen to have an awful lot of people running round the United States of America who are not only certifiably nuts but feel entitled as certifiable nuts to do something to call their condition to the attention of the public.

A.A.: It is logical, then, that a belief in equality of opportunity and the rest should lead, under certain circumstances, to a belief in the equality of opportunity to express one's psychopathic tendencies. It's also logical that the sheer size and mobility and loneliness of America should produce violence; in such conditions you have to make an extreme gesture in order to convince yourself that you exist. But apart from the psychological and geographical factors, there is also a historical and political tradition of violence in the country. Two writers describe it. First, Ralph Ellison, the Negro novelist and author of one of the finest post-war works of fiction, *Invisible Man*:

ELLISON: There is in the country a tradition of violence which comes from its frontier aspects. It also comes from its ceaseless mobility; it comes from the clashes of group against group. You know we had something called the Civil War, which was an armed conflict which had a traumatic effect upon us. But what followed was the *civil* war. And that civil war, the war of society, the war of group against group, is built into the American thing. This produces violence. And it isn't necessarily bad, because it's what happens when you put so many different people together in a country and you have a political system which depends upon the pressure of groups.

A.A.: Now Joseph Frank, the literary critic:

FRANK: I think that, in the American experience, you have to keep in mind that violence is closer even historically to the American imagination and American reality than is the case in Europe. The Indian wars ended less than a hundred years ago and the archetypal American experience – the experience all of us have had in the movies as children – was exactly that of lawlessness as a threat to the whole order of the state and of the social order. And this has become a part of the American myth. It's romantic as well as being dangerous.

I still think we have to keep in mind that as children it was always law and order that won out, and this was the experience which impressed our imagination. Everything that was evil and threatening was an undermining of the social order. And when we saw all of this in Texas as a reality, as adults, it was more than we could stand; and all the expressions of anguish and shock are a result of this.

A.A.: Now the peculiar anguish and shock of the intellectuals over the events in Dallas has, I think, at least two sources. First, they not only identified a little with the President who was shot; they also, grudgingly and fearfully, identified with his assassins. This is a private theory, for which I got precious little support in America. Nevertheless, there is a curious fact that when the *New York Review of Books* produced a memorial number for President Kennedy, well over half of it was devoted to Oswald. I suspect that this may be because a large proportion of the contributors had, in their youth in the thirties, been alienated left-wing sympathizers. It is equally probable that their families objected to this out of the very roots of their respectability. So, to some tiny extent, they may have identified with Oswald – despite his paranoid, half-baked Marxism. Whilst Jack Ruby, despite his dabbling with the underworld and the police, had enough family-loving, synagogue-going, pop piety and muddled idealism to seem like everybody's Uncle Max from Brooklyn. The Dallas affair, then, was like a terrible, absurd, Oedipal slaying in reverse.

This, as I say, is a private theory. I wouldn't want to push it too far. What is less questionable is that some of the intellectuals had been consciously dabbling with the problem of violence. It was a response to the cosiness of the Eisenhower administration, to the recognition of violent upheaval in the Civil Rights demonstrations and the concurrent debates on the 'invisible poor': those forty-odd million who live below the economic water-line in the U.S.A. So the idea of violence became a valid existential response to the deep unease of so much American life. The main promoter of this idea was Norman Mailer. Podhoretz analyses his concern with it:

PODHORETZ: The only intellectual I take seriously who could be said to be involved in anything like a cult of violence is Norman Mailer. I don't know anybody else whom I specially regard who's been deeply concerned with this problem. I think it's crude to describe Mailer's interest in violence as cultish. Mailer's belief is not that violence is in itself a good thing or anything of that sort, but that the amount of violence in American life is a direct consequence of the repression of spontaneity all over the place, plus the increasing alienation of the senses in this kind of advanced industrial, urban society, plus the lack of occasion for the direct expression of emotion, which is, you know, another form of suppression. It isn't sexual, but it involves the whole being of a man. So it's not a question of pursuing violence for its own sake so much as recognizing its presence and the extent to which it trembles so constantly and ubiquitously below the surface of the life we lead.

But if one is aware that this kind of thing is happening to one – that is to say that the civilized crust *is* a crust, and that there are storms below that have no easy outlet – if one is conscious of this, in a way for example that the British seemed not to be conscious of it for a very long time, one is then stuck with a kind of responsibility towards oneself and towards truth. You see? And how do you resolve this contradiction, how do you live with it without yourself becoming violent, without joining the barbarians? Nobody quite knows. This is not an American problem, it's a problem that's endemic, it seems to me, to modern life and to highly urbanized industrial civilizations, especially those with a Puritan tradition.

A.A.: Now Mailer's existential views had crystallized in a more-or-less admiring way around Kennedy, the man who in the war had gone through great danger and survived, who had taken calculated risks with his life (for example, his highly chancy back operation which could easily have been a killer), who had, in his physical presence, a certain inspiring – and inspiriting – beauty and power. In his book, *The Presidential Papers*, Mailer labels Kennedy 'the existential hero'. He also described the assassination to me in much the same terms.

MAILER: The awful thing about the assassination of Kennedy was that when he went down to Dallas and travelled through Dallas in a car without a glass top, I think he was taking a calculated existential risk. After all, he was a bold man. Afterwards, everyone said: 'Well, he owed it to us to put on the glass dome; he shouldn't have taken that sort of chance.' Actually, I think what he felt was: 'Yes, Dallas is a violent city, but it's not that violent, and I'm going to go down there and travel through in an open car, and after I travel through in an open car, everyone's going to realize that Dallas is not that violent, and that the race situation is not as bad as people claim it is.' You see? Because, after all, he was always defining the nature of our reality for us by his actions, which is, I think, his claim on greatness as a president: he helped establish a sense of reality for us, a very imaginative, interesting, contradictory sense of reality, rather than being some large vapid figure of authority whom one believed in, as some sort of secular pope. Of course, he lost on that gamble; and what it meant to Americans was that indeed our buried life was far more violent than we thought it was.

A.A.: If Kennedy defined the nature of reality for the American intellectuals, he also provided a kind of ideal. They could look into that mirror and feel that things weren't so bad, for there was the image of the beautiful Kennedys, with their intelligence, stylishness, toughness, and enlightened glow. So the nature of reality began to seem, despite everything, full of possibilities. The hero had merely to brave the risk of violence. But Dallas changed all that. It was not merely that buried violence proved stronger than enlightened heroism. It was also that the faces of violence – Oswald and Ruby – were vaguely familiar. The intellectuals looked in the mirror again and saw their own ids staring stupidly and violently back at them. And this is something they had never foreseen when they explored their fantasies of violence for their existential possibilities. For the fantasies were not only theoretically health-giving and even possibly creative, they were also, on a lower level, flattering: you adopted the hipster stance and looked – well, like Marlon Brando or Charlie Parker, maybe even like Kennedy. Then suddenly you discovered that you didn't look like that at all; you looked like Oswald or Ruby – crude, dangerous, a bit mad.

Put it another way: heroism is always a gamble; the hero can easily become a tragic hero, particularly in a time as violent and unstable as ours. And if the hero is an existential hero, then he is inevitably vulnerable to the unpredictability of existence. That is, for every hero there is always an inverted anti-hero; for every Kennedy an Oswald or Ruby; 'every calculated existential risk', as Mailer calls it, risks also the absurd – even if, as it happened in Dallas, the size and effect of the absurd is that of a major international tragedy.

KEMPTON: It's easy for me to say that I am not responsible for the House Un-American Activities Committee. But how can I say that I'm not responsible for another American – precisely the private man that I am – who shoots – well, I keep saying the President of the United States, but let's try to make it a little more domestic than that – shoots an absolutely charming man whom everyone who knew enjoyed and for whom all of us had this immense affection? Now how can I say that I am not responsible for this? How can I be alienated from this particular act, whether the assassin is a Bircher, a communist, or almost anything else? I've got to struggle to be alienated from this.

You really do have to swim upstream against something in order to swim well. Now I'm talking like an American, but it's true. There is a lot in American life against which one should swim upstream, but it is possible to continue to go downstream while thinking you are swimming upstream, if you choose the proper issues. The truth of the matter is that we are at a point in this country where the Central Europeans were maybe forty years ago. We are beginning to understand that what you have to swim upstream against is yourself. And this is a terrible thing to deal with. That's why we are so insistent on judgement and trial, on blaming somebody else, hating poor Barry Goldwater, hating the John Birch Society, hating the Fair Play for Cuba Committee, hating Jack Ruby more than you do whoever it was who assassinated the President – and I don't know who it was. But somehow or other, finding somebody to blame. Because we can talk about the absurd all the time, yet it's not in our tradition that anything that's absurd can exist. And the thing to do, I think – the problem that we have – is to face the absurd and not give way to it.

6. The Intellectuals and Society

To begin with the most obvious and important point: America is, in my experience, the only country in the world which is, for better and for worse, squarely, uncompromisingly in the twentieth century. Most of the Western European countries are only reluctantly there: England and France, for example, remain emotionally around nineteen hundred and ten, thoroughly industrialized but dreaming still of times past – witness the cold houses, the half-hearted architecture, the awful roads, the boring class distinctions, the gently good manners. Russia, I suppose, is about eighteen seventy: politically the industrial revolution has taken hold, but its benefits have not yet spread out much to the general public. Poland, under its patina of sophistication, still keeps the social habits of the late-eighteenth-century squirearchy. Hungary and Yugoslavia are almost ready for the Renaissance. China, apparently, is just raising itself out of the Dark Ages, whilst a country like Albania is still tribal.

But America is the real modern thing: a gleaming, air-conditioned, brightly packaged, technological mass society devoted, with startling single-mindedness, to making life easy. Nearly everything either has or aspires to a certain surface efficiency and glimmer, an air of steel, glass, electronic device, speed and instant chic. Every single citizen assumes his right to the benefits of the mass-production society; his share, that is, of the smart, cheap clothes and the machines – of the cars, ice-boxes, TV sets. For example, one of the two great moral and political questions facing the country at present is that of poverty: the fact that one person in four in this huge, wealthy country gets by on less than what is considered to be a decent subsistence wage. The problem is certainly a real one – in some areas acutely so – and has given rise first to a good deal of indignation and now to a full-scale political-economic programme to change the situation. But if the presidential war against poverty is finally won, everyone, from the top of society to the bottom, will by European standards be middle-class. Even now everyone *looks* middle-class. In *The Other America*, the book which first brought the problem to the public's attention, Michael Harrington wrote: 'Clothes make the poor invisible too: America has the best-dressed poverty the world has ever known.'

This paradoxical stylishness – style in the absence of substance, style in the place of means – relates to something more than poverty. It is also typical somehow of America's modernity, and it is at the root of the problem we too have to face as we move fully into the twentieth century. It is a matter of coming to terms with a new kind of reality, a reality in which style and being, surface and inward awareness, appearance and feeling are utterly and, apparently, irreconcilably at odds. We are beginning to have a way of life so elegantly designed that it is impermeable, it leaves no room for human muddle.

The terms of the problem are already clichés: most of them boil down to the question of the conflict between the individual and mass society, human effort and the machine, et cetera. It's all old hat, even over here. But in America it's not merely old hat, it's unavoidable. There is nowhere else to look or to go, and nothing else to do. It faces you everywhere in the most seductive disguises.

For example, during my stay there recently, I spent a good deal of time flying in jet liners from one city to another. It's at once the easiest and more forceful way of feeling what it's like to belong to the twentieth century. You are carried miles up at a ludicrous speed in a cocoon of bottled air and bottled music, while shiny, mass-produced hostesses ply you with the food and the pilot intones his soothing creed: 'Sit back, relax and enjoy your flight.' When it's over, you are decanted into airports of smooth glass and aluminium and swept whisperingly along super highways into the cities. It's marvellous, imposing –

even, in a way, rather touching. But it's also unreal, a bit impossible. All that tailored steel and glass fits too closely together. There seems scarcely room, even at the interstices, to lead your own messy, inefficient life. So you get a slightly ghostly feeling, as though existence itself had become automated and you were reduced to just another hole in the computer's punch-card.

Of course, it doesn't quite work out like that. The planes go wrong, the schedules don't tally, the seats in the elegant waiting-rooms are as hard on the bottom as those in any English branch-line station, and the cities, when you finally settle in, are reassuringly filthy. As the Americans are the first to tell you. Here, for example, is the novelist, Herbert Gold:

GOLD : All this smooth-running machinery is actually not very smooth-running. I have an automobile with power steering, power windows, power brakes, and the power's always going off. I spend half the morning sweeping water out of my smooth-fitting car. And the same with those wonderful airplanes. I lose my baggage every other trip. So you spend only five hours getting across country, and you spend another twelve hours trying to find your valise.

A.A. : Total efficiency is as much an unattained ideal as total democratic equality. Mercifully, perhaps. But if no one ever really expected the twentieth century to work, everyone expects it to look as if it might. Whatever the reality, the appearance must be at once compelling and quietening, stimulating and tranquillizing.

The trouble is, the tranquillizers aren't really effective. Among the intellectuals particularly, the great and available comfort of the country produces not ease and a sense of fulfilment but anxiety. They feel it, according to Irving Howe, as a kind of lobotomy:

HOWE : A lobotomy which removes the symptoms of your disorder, of your anger, but necessarily can't get at the

E   129

roots of the disorder or the anger. So the trouble seethes beneath the surface. You meet many people in this country who by every conventional, ordinary standard ought to be very happy: they're successful, they have good families, they have some money, they do work that means something – and yet, one knows among one's friends, in one's own life, that there is a vast quantity of unhappiness prevalent through the middle and intellectual classes. I think this might be a good way of putting it: we have a society in which any number of people are contented but unhappy.

A.A.: This unhappiness, this sense of a deep and continual unease, is what the intellectuals more or less prize as their alienation. In the previous chapter, the problem came up in analysing their relations with Kennedy. But it extends more widely and deeply than that. In a sense, alienation is a geographical inevitability in America. The country is so vast and so various, and the pace so ruthless, that the sensitive person is of necessity pushed in on himself, his identity not so much swallowed up by the machine as lost in the desert. As Auden says:

> Some think they're strong, some think they're smart,
> Like butterflies they're pulled apart,
> America can break your heart.

The sheer physical presence itself of this endless, indifferent country produces a kind of threatening yet seductive loneliness. But this too can sometimes be a source of creative power. Witness Robert Lowell:

LOWELL: I feel that it's a very naked country; the sort of flesh that goes on the skeleton and the nervous system that works it is very meagre. This is such a cliché I sort of blush to utter it, but you go from New York to London and they're two cities in many ways much alike and maybe they're essentially alike; but the superficial difference hits you terribly hard: that you can't touch a stone in London that doesn't point backwards into history, while even for an American city, New York seems to have no past. Yet it's the only city that sort of provides an intellectual human continuum to live in. You don't have to live in New York, of course. Many people loathe living in it. But still if you removed it, you'd be cutting out the heart of American culture. Yet it's a heart with no past: the New York of fifty years ago is utterly gone and there are no landmarks that are a record of the city. It doesn't point back into the past, so it has that sheer presence – a great sheer feeling of utter freedom and so forth. And then when one thinks back a little bit, it seems all confused and naked.

A.A. : The image of America as a great powerful ship driving into the future, with its past closing up continually behind it like a wake, not only has a certain imaginative appeal to the Americans, it also defines their reality and their confusion. 'A heart with no past.' It would be more or less impossible, say, for an American critic as crucially important and influential as F. R. Leavis is over here, to hanker, as the doctor did, for the moral strength and sense of community of a pre-Industrial Revolution society. For in a sense there is no pre-industrial America, or none that is in the least either relevant or viable now. In fact, the U.S.A. is the one country in the world which is unequivocally a product of the Industrial Revolution. The settling of the continent and the development of its immense powers would not have been possible if the men who gradually spread westward had not been ready to use every new technique as it was evolved. Even now the country would have little collective identity if it weren't for the continued exploitation of all the techniques of mass communication: television, radio, telephone and aeroplane.

But dissociation from the past and continual commitment to the present as it evolves into the future means that the United States tends to look for its securities not in tradition but in power – in the force of the present rather than that of the past.

LOWELL: We're a country founded on a Constitution. That makes us rather different from the usual country that's founded on a history, a culture. We were founded on a Declaration, on a Constitution, on Principles. We always have the sort of idea of saving the world, and that comes close to perhaps destroying the world. Suddenly it's as though this really terrible nightmare, I think, had come true; that we are suddenly in a position where we might destroy the world, and that's very closely allied to saving it. We might blow up Cuba to save ourselves and then the whole world would blow up. Yet it would come in the guise of an idealistic stroke. It is what is unreal about America and what's noble about America. Violence and idealism have some connexion. I remember reading Henry Adams's *History of Jefferson and Madison*. It's a rather sceptical history, far from idealizing America (though it's different from Adams's later position). I noticed the strange pride that Adams takes in American gunnery – it's almost wild Western; that the American ships shot better than the English ships and that Andrew Jackson's artillery shot better than the British artillery. All that had some great symbolic significance to him. We seem to be a very sheer country. I mean power is something everyone must have, because the country's powerful. The ideal isn't real unless it's somehow backed by power. Robert Frost was very much criticized for his remark about poetry and power: 'We must have more of both.' Well, he seemed to rejoice in that. But in a way I feel it's our curse, that we can't disentangle those two things.

A.A.: This feeling that power has a kind of physical presence in the country – as though it were as palpably there as are the prairies, the deserts and the Rockies – is for some writers at once inspiring and a bit terrifying.

MAILER: The terror, I believe, does have a relation to a twentieth-century phenomenon: that is, the slow totalitarianization of everything. If one starts looking at modern architecture, for example, I think it's the perfect expression of the totalitarian *geist*, enormous power without detail, commitment, curiosity, mystery, or variety. One just has an enormous flat statement of a power. After all, every large building represents more than a few wealthy real-estate operators; it also represents the social process that made all that possible. And this terror is precisely, I think, the sort of terror that impelled Orwell to write *Nineteen Eighty-Four*. He was really the first to talk about the totalitarianization of the world not as a political phenomenon, but as a psychic, indeed even a spiritual phenomenon. If one can talk hypothetically of a God: it's as if this God were being invaded by disease, as if the very substance of everyone's being was being captured by a subtle and insidious machine. The buried shape of this terror is that the very substance of being, if I can use that existential notion, is being devoured, absorbed, altered – perhaps in some cold, dead way, being destroyed. This sensation is a part of American paranoia; because we feel these things quicker than anyone else does. In a sense we're a nation without a skin; certainly, *vis-à-vis* the French, we are a nation without a skin.

Of course, one can argue that a great many Americans have an enormous pride in precisely all these phenomena: the modern buildings, the jet planes, super highways, and so forth. But what I would argue back is that what characterizes all totalitarian movements is that they're swollen with pride, and empty pride, a pride which cannot take in more than a few particular details. One of the essences of totalitarianism is that it enjoys precisely destroying the particular, it loathes the source of the particular. The intimate nature of totalitarianism is that you put saccharine in your tea instead of sugar. I think at the very heart of totalitarianism is the desire to cheat life: to have the sweet taste without putting on the weight.

A. A. : It's important to realize that Mailer is not using the word 'totalitarianism' in the same sense as Hannah Arendt used it in her great work on the subject. In Mailer's vocabulary the word has almost nothing to do with the régimes of Hitler and Stalin and everything to do with massive scale and intricate proliferation of a society which cares for the individual – that is, sets him up in great comfort – at the same time as it sucks him of his individuality. According to Irving Howe, this existential threat has become a social reality for a large proportion of the more comfortable citizens:

HOWE: One of the things that I've noticed in travelling around the country is that there's a new kind of social feeling – a social sentiment – that you find especially in the *nouveau riche* American middle class, the kind of people who have made their money in the last fifteen or twenty years. To them the whole idea of modern history, the whole idea of a threat from Europe, is taken in personal terms. Not only does it threaten the country, or the community, it seems to them to be a danger to their own money, to their own recently acquired status – to their swimming pools and their double cars and their garages and things of that sort. It's as if they want to withdraw from the whole of modern history, to pull out of all the threats and dangers. They go on the rather childlike assumption that simply by making a decision, that simply by determining to pull away, it can be done.

There's something else that I've noticed: a new kind of selfishness, such as one doesn't usually associate with American life; a feeling that if somebody is poor it's because that person has moral faults, because that person somehow doesn't live up to the clean, good, genteel standards of the American middle class. Previously the whole tradition, by and large, of American liberalism or progressivism has been that of social sympathy, of identifying with victims, with the poor. Now you find a very hard and rigid and brusque and nasty kind of feeling among middle-class people in this country; a feeling that they have theirs, they found their way to success, they've got their pile and those on the bottom – of whom there are still, after all, millions in America – those on the bottom had just as well be quiet or be kept down. They don't want to hear about troubles. They don't want to hear about other people's suffering, other people's misery. It's a little bit like the kind of ideology of social Darwinism that we had in the late nineteenth century in America, namely the mechanical application or misapplication of Darwinian theory to social life; that is, that those who are competent succeed, and if someone fails, that's evidence that he isn't competent to make it in the race of life. A new version of this occurs in the American middle class these days. It's very dismal, unattractive. It's morally unattractive, and it's socially unattractive. It's the source of what is called Radical Right politics in America, and I think it's much more dangerous.

A. A. : Perhaps this new indifference is a kind of psychic or social equivalent of the forces Lowell and Mailer were trying to define: the physical sheerness of the country, the brutal power of the architecture and the social machine. It appears at its most deadening and dangerous in its political disguises: Goldwaterism, for example, and the even more viciously monolithic groupings on the extremist fringe. It appears, too, in the curiously brutal insentience of casual social exchange – in buses and subways, walking or driving – a matter not so much of brusqueness as of a feeling, exuded by so many, of utter indifference to everyone else.

Yet this disengaged, slightly violent, dangerous quality can be seductive, in its own style – particularly for the visiting foreigner who has towards it all none of the responsibility and guilt of the native American. Indeed, the other, less shady side of the power thing is oddly optimistic and positive, less threatening than stimulating. The first impact America makes is one of immense energy and sense of possibility. Great roads are being stretched across the country, great buildings are continually going up (Mies van der Rohe's Seagram Building is, for my money, one of the most beautiful pieces of architecture in the world). The best artists and thinkers paint and write with a kind of fierce ambition quite unusual elsewhere: they seem genuinely concerned to make it new on their own most imaginative terms. There is a sense of risk and energy which is quite unlike our own fatigued timidity. Even the Americans think so, in their less gloomy moments. For example, I suggested to the novelist, Ralph Ellison, that the immense impact of America's modernity was in part due to the fact that it's the only country which has, in its buildings, really assimilated abstract art into its daily pattern of living. He replied:

ELLISON: It could do that because it had no real tradition of its own and it's had to play it by ear from the very beginning. It's always worked towards the functional, towards the clean cut and efficient. So when we can get the combinations working together – that is, a sponsor, a client who is willing to pay the money, an architect who has taste and a sense of the adventurous, and who is following the best principles which have been evolved both in this country and in Europe – you get something like the Seagram Building or the Lever Building or the new Chase Manhattan Plaza. It *is* exciting. After living in Rome for a couple of years, I came back to New York and I felt this terrific release of energy. The visual impact of New York was just tremendous.

A.A.: Yet this marvellous creative energy has its inverted social-mirror image in a kind of despair.

HOWE: We ought to say a word about the new phrase that's begun to be used by some social writers in America, which I think very important. People speak no longer only of a working class, or an oppressed class, they now speak of an under class. What they mean by an under class is those millions of people who are beneath social visibility, whom you don't see very much when you walk around in the streets as a tourist in the cities, who are hidden away in the corners and the crevices of American society, but who really are extremely numerous, who don't get along economically, who don't rise on the social ladder, who don't send their children to college, who are, so to say, permanently depressed, who don't even belong to the trade unions, because they're beneath that. They do menial jobs or part-time work, or they're on relief, or they scrounge along in some way or other. These people are beyond the amelioration of the ordinary social steps that are taken in this country, and they form a potentially very explosive layer in the population, a layer of potential violence, but also of great passivity too. The passivity and the violence tend to go together. When you think about the existence of millions of such people in American society, who are very seldom known of in foreign countries, then you may see why some of the better novelists in America in the last twenty years have not shared in the mood of American celebration, of national self-congratulation which has seized the country, and why the better writers often have been critical and disturbed and upset by what was going on in this country.

HARDWICK: One of the things about living in a country like America where there's a good deal of prosperity – although apparently we have less than we thought – is that you can always imagine how much better it could be. There's a good deal of guilt over well-being; people feel guilty because America is so ugly and the cars are so hideous and television is so bad. It creates a feeling of shame, when you think they might so easily be better. But still, the fact remains that the chaos of our society we feel is totally unnecessary. The pain that still exists for a large number of people does actually seem to be unnecessary. So there is a good deal of frustration for a writer in feeling that these things are unnecessary. I mean the high cost of medical care and the bad medical treatment of poor people and the bad education. These are all just truisms – everyone knows this. But still, you're very frustrated. . . .

A.A.: Perhaps it is in this sense of inadequacy that the roots of the intellectuals' alienation can be found.

PODHORETZ: It seems to me that the intellectual is alienated by definition: at least in my definition of the intellectual, the word 'alienation' would come into the first sentence, maybe the first paragraph anyhow, because I define intellectual in something like prophetic terms: he is someone committed to a vision of what I once rather cornily called a decent life on this planet. We shall probably never have a decent life on this planet, so there will always be a gap between those ideals and values to which the intellectuals by nature ought to be committed and the social reality. This is why I'm concerned about the mobilization of the intellectual community, because it does tend, by itself, to subvert the intellectual's sense of his function. And his function is to speak for all the dissatisfied impulses in man and all the dissatisfied classes in society, and all restlessness and longing, all the visionary traditions. I call them 'traditions' because there is nothing new to be said about what a decent life on this planet would look like. This has been defined by the tradition of modernity.

A.A.: In principle, Podhoretz is no doubt right. The trouble is that the theory doesn't quite fit the realities of the intellectual's life in America. Here is the late R. P. Blackmur, one of the most distinguished American literary critics:

BLACKMUR: I would suppose that one of the really perennial thorns in the side of the intellectual's flesh, one that cannot be pulled out, is that there is no way under any economy any modern society has had whereby that intellectual can be a going member of the economy. He'll always tend towards being a member of an intellectual proletariat, if you like to put it that way. I was thinking of Toynbee's definition of the proletarian as a man who was in but not of his society. And the intellectual is very likely to feel that way. This is what many people call alienation. But I would suppose it was a fairly regular condition that will be ameliorated one way or another by different means from time to time. As in this country, any intellectual who doesn't insist on going to gaol can get himself some sort of support for his work, no matter how alien to the normal purposes of society that work is. As I believe every European knows, there's never been such an age for patronage as the American patronage now available, and on such a wide base.

A.A.: The paradox, then, of the intellectuals' position is this: another well-known critic sums it up:

MARK SCHORER: Isn't it true that a good deal of creative energy is generated by alienation and that energy can continue to operate, as in many writers I can think of – writers who have been honoured, showered with awards, written successful works, whose works sold and so on – that the motivation still comes of a sense of not belonging in a situation that no longer really exists.

A.A.: The situation is, then, rather as Norman Mailer described it. The vast, hungry machinery of modern technological society sucks individuals in and swallows them whole. But its indifference is not necessarily malicious; instead, it kills with kindness. On this nearly everyone agrees.

HOFSTADTER: I think another utterly insoluble dilemma in which the intellectual lives in an absorptive society like contemporary America, is the apparatus that is set up to receive and at least apparently recognize his dissenting notions or his outrageous sensibilities. What used to be quite marginal and on the border-lines of pornography, the kind of thing for which publishers and writers used to have to fight very strong agitational and legal battles, is now to be had on practically any American news-stand. Radical notions create celebrities. Angry young men become quickly saturated with money and attention for being angry. And there is simply no way in which an intellectual who has the least bit of this kind of exposure can go on nursing his own sense of specialness and building up the bile that goes with his grievance.

HARDWICK: It's this vast machine of publicity that really cannot be offended. I mean you can't even write about sex any more, and they accept that. They accept everything. Which is all right because they have to feed these machines, these papers – *Time* magazine, *Newsweek*, everything. They cannot really afford to ignore anything, everything is absorbed and accepted. There isn't an *avant-garde*.

A.A.: The problem then is this: writers want to be against the *status quo*, but it can't be done. The *status quo* changes too quickly for them. And in changing it buys them off: it salves their wounds with money; it stuffs those cultural gaps with hard cash. Someone who has certainly had to face this problem in his own work is one of America's most important novelists, Saul Bellow:

BELLOW: There's hardly anything that can be invented by any American rebel which won't be incorporated into the general cultural effort of the country and be richly rewarded; it's one of the paradoxes of American life. A man may write a protest novel, a novel about the poor, and find himself, having done so, a millionaire. This has been the lot of quite a few American writers. There isn't a writer in the United States who doesn't feel proud of his rebellious record. The only trouble is that his rebellion doesn't have a great deal of content, and I sometimes wonder whether this is because American society doesn't relegate all its critics to a sort of infantile or childish situation. That is, to say, 'You may say what you like as long as you have no power or authority. Go right ahead; we're perfectly glad to have you, the more extreme the better.' It's a positive encouragement of extremism. I think it's commercially stimulated, too, because people are looking for new things to goose the new middle class with; I mean the new bureaucratic class which is having such a good time, and the executive class, the newly developed scientific group, the administrators, and all the rest of these have to be entertained. They turn to intellectuals for their entertainment and also for a certain degree of seriousness. But it's not the sort of seriousness that has any sort of applicability socially.

A.A. : This way of benevolently absorbing the intellectuals and amiably deadening the impact of their protest – smilingly castrating them, if you will – is nothing very new in American life:

The ordinary citizen will not struggle energetically against [the innovator] – sometimes they will even applaud him; but they do not follow him. To his vehemence they secretly oppose their inertia, to his revolutionary tendencies their conservative interests, their homely tastes to his adventurous passions, their good sense to the flights of his genius, to his poetry their prose. With immense exertion, he raises them for an instant, but they speedily escape from him, and fall back, as it were, by their own weight. He strains himself to rouse the indifferent and distracted multitude, and finds at last that he is reduced to impotence, not because he is conquered, but because he is alone.

So de Tocqueville in 1835. In a way, the innovator's loneliness today is increased by his success.

GOLD : The writers are now something like movie stars in America. It means you get paid for giving lectures; it means you get paid for doing adaptations, paid for appearing at banquets. It doesn't mean that your work is necessarily taken much more seriously. Maybe it's better to be invited to speak at universities than to be totally ignored. It's certainly better on a practical level. But I think it produces a kind of despair in writers who are, some of us, attacked by the critics as popular successes before we've enjoyed that popular success. There is a kind of silent fame that many American writers have.

A.A.: In order to beat this 'silent fame', a great number of American artists and intellectuals are depressingly ready to adjust themselves and their work to the demands of the art-consuming society. (Indeed, the artists and intellectuals form one of the few classes which is not likely to be made redundant by automation; on the contrary, the demand for their work will increase as automation gives more leisure to the rest of society.) But the speed at which the publicity machine keeps fashionable taste right up to date makes it easy for the artists to feel way out, whilst being in fact way in. Zero Mostel, to my mind America's most brilliant comedian, also a painter and connoisseur of art, gives an example of this self-adjusting mechanism.

MOSTEL: You can't afford to put anything on. If I were to say: 'I want to do *Timon of Athens* tomorrow. Damn everybody, I think this play should be seen. It has a message for all Romans' – I couldn't do it. It's impossible to do because I haven't got the wherewithal, the money. It's all money, it is a commercial problem. They know that what cheers them up is that safe approach to the theatre. Therefore comes that way a formula. One day they make a big deal; they want to do *Waiting for Godot* by Beckett. They say 'limited engagement of eight weeks' just because they won't let it go on more than eight weeks. And they will make the play suffer by doing it in such a way that it's a little bit burlesque and not to the point of the play.

Those people who get the modern paintings, they put up

in an academy immediately about what a painting should be. Painting now is to fling a pot of paint on the canvas; no matter who flings it. Now, you know if someone flings a piece of paint on a canvas, he still has some control; others don't have control. But the guy who buys it thinks that all pots of paint flung at the canvas are good. Therefore anybody who steps on or rolls the model in a piece of canvas, or produces a squirt gun . . . I was with a very famous painter and we were standing there talking when a blob of his paint suddenly sank. There was too much varnish in it. So I said: 'Your paint is dripping.' So he said: 'I mean it to be that way.' He's full of milakee; he didn't mean it to be that way.

A.A.: Yet this deft adjustment to fashion doesn't necessarily come easily.

HOWE: I was away from New York for several years and, reading the intellectual journals from a distance, I had the feeling that things were, from my own sort of socialist view, getting better. Mainly that there was a turn to the left, a greater social awareness, a growth of radicalism as you looked at the journals. But when I came back to New York I had a disappointed feeling that, in a way, it didn't make much difference what was being said in the intellectual journals and in the quarterlies and the weeklies, because the style of life, the kind of conduct that people lived, wasn't changed by their opinion. In the early fifties, they could turn towards a kind of conservatism and now in the sixties move leftward a little bit, but the drift of life remains pretty much the same. What they say is all too much a matter of writing an article, rather than conducting a way of life. I don't want to make this seem crude, because these are serious people that we're talking about, and very gifted people too. It isn't a matter of their selling out for comfort; it's that you slowly drift into a certain way of existence, a way of existence that doesn't depend even on making so very much money – since intellectuals don't make that much money – but on finding the easier, more comfortable way out of things. Another point: thirty years ago there were organized movements on the left, which were a channel for the expression of political sentiments. Today there are no movements, so that you have to do personally what is done by parties and organizations elsewhere.

A.A. : There are two points here. First, the ineffectuality of one's protest and the degree of one's conformity to the standards of middle-class comfort are more painful now because the thirties are still a potent memory: that is, most intellectuals can remember a time when individual protest and political action seemed related. Second, when a political gesture is transformed into an existential gesture, it increases the individual's sense of loneliness and practical impotence.

RAHV : Sex has also become innocuous. They can allow writers to be as clinical, as explicit about the description of sexual intercourse as they please, because they are afraid of only one thing: communism. Sex is not political; in fact, it can be used in a political situation as tense as this one between East and West. Sex in the West – that is, sexual explicitness – is harmless: who cares what people do in bed? What they care about is what they think politically, and that if they think the wrong thoughts it will endanger the system. But what they do privately in their bedroom has nothing whatever to do with their privileged position in society.

The lack of opportunity to externalize pressures in terms of political organization and activity and idealism means that at the worst intellectuals turn back into themselves and begin to exaggerate the values of private life. Naturally, there is this tremendous overpowering exaggeration of the sexual relationship of which the novelist has taken advantage. Society puts no inhibitions upon them so far as publishing whatever they please so long as the sexual problem is handled apart from the social one. It is simply a question of private enjoyment or repression or happiness. So long as it's private, it has no political resonance or reference.

A.A. : I personally disagree with this. For example, Norman Mailer seems to be testing privately the possibilities of life in contemporary America in a way which does have distinct political resonance. Even so, it's certainly true that political protest has become to some extent existential and internal; and it's equally true that all protest is blandly assimilated. The result of this, I think, is that the intellectuals begin *to doubt the reality of their experience.*

KEMPTON : I've always heard how much the intellectual was alienated in the United States. I don't think he really was. There was a general feeling that we were being chased. But actually this is a very comfortable country to dissent in. So many of us, I think, were socialist in the thirties. We didn't realize at the time it was a form of social climbing, that it was a way of sort of getting ahead, and also acquiring certain skills which were useful to the structure of society. For example, we explained the Labour Movement to the employers and by the time we finished explaining it they had nothing to fear from the Labour Movement. We then turned around and explained they had nothing to fear from us. This long period of McCarthyism, for example, was largely spent in explaining that we really weren't that dangerous and we really weren't engaged in trying to overthrow the government, and we were also purer than the Communists. There was a strong tendency in the United States to serve the Communists up as hostages to respectability. Of course there were people who suffered terribly from McCarthy. But most of the people who made the choice of testifying for the House Un-American Activities Committee were choosing whether to stay and be honoured in a confiscatory tax bracket or whether to work in a more modest area. To suggest that this had something to do with having your feet cooked by the tortures of the Inquisition was fairly silly.

The whole Communist experience in the United States was as though somebody had gone off somewhere to some sort of London School of Economics seminar, in which from time to time schoolteachers came in and cracked your wrist if you fell asleep, and from time to time you had to clean up the place and get the cigarette butts and everything else out. You went through this unreal kind of experience, then you came out and talked about this as though it had been an experience. What you did was to identify yourself, one way or another, either with the people who shot Trotskyites or the Trotskyites who were shot, or the people of the Spanish War who were shot. But you identified their experience with the business of sitting at a party meeting and discussing how many leaflets you could put out tomorrow morning, or various forms of disguising yourself and so on. And you thought this was real. You know, nothing ever happened. There were no experiences. So maybe you left the party and somebody would not speak to you the next day. Well, this is a bearable situation. I mean, if you get divorce, your former father-in-law doesn't speak to you. This is a rather limited part of experience, you know. But the thing that I'm trying to say is that we were continually taking things that were really not experiences and pretending they were. This is a terrible American problem.

A.A.: Again, there are two issues here. First, the wealth, comfort and amiably monolithic readiness of American society to make things easy for its rebels all combine to strip rebellion and protest of meaning. So the unhappiness and alienation of the protesting intellectuals seem either disproportionate or totally unreal.

HARDWICK: A society like this makes it rather difficult to live out your dissent. It's a verbal thing. I mean, you work and you're well paid and there are some subtle restrictions, certainly. But still, it's rather hard to make your day-to-day living in any way conform to your stated despair and worry and dissatisfaction with American life. You feel that an intelligent American, but not what you'd call an intellectual American, really finds it almost impossible to take seriously the deep alienation – to use all these rather tired words – and disaffection of these highbrows. He truly doesn't know what you're talking about. He feels that this is an indulgence and a falsehood, that you don't really feel that way. That's a real question: do the intellectuals really feel that way? It's much more complicated than it seems. How much do these attitudes affect one's actual living? How much can you live them out? Your attitude of feeling alien from the society, or not accepting its values, and keeping in your mind that other societies – I mean contemporary societies in Europe and so on – have things to offer that we don't. But the important thing is that I think even poor Americans – taxi-drivers or farmers – would be astonished at the sort of despair that's in the highbrow magazines. I mean, as to whether it's meant to be taken seriously or not.

A.A.: Considering the easy lives that many of the American intellectuals live, some of their European counterparts might well share the astonishment of those taxi-drivers. But there's a second point to be made from Kempton's argument, one that also relates to Miss Hardwick's: there exists in America a huge, more or less unrecognized mechanism not merely for assimilating protest but also for buttressing everybody from the realities of their experience. I suggested earlier that in order to be tolerable, those great, throbbing, impersonal machines to which everyone entrusts their lives – the jet liners and the business corporations. the skyscrapers and the nuclear armies – all have to come with built-in tranquillizers. The most potent of these tranquillizers is language.

Consider, for example, that famous American friendliness, that instantaneous, ease-promoting first-naming of anyone and everyone. It either arouses in Europeans a certain easy and unreal warmth; or it frightens them out of their wits; or it makes them suspect hypocrisy. It is, in fact, none of these.

ELLISON: It's true conversation's become formalized in a certain way which is rather tricky. Immediately you go into a strange town somebody is going to start calling you by your first name. I'm not just speaking as a Negro; this happens to everybody. And it is generally understood – except by very naïve people – that this is not a gesture of real friendship but of a stylized friendship. It's a convenience and it does allow the individual some protection.

A.A. : This casual social ease, then, may be a manifestation of the American national genius for remembering names, but it is not necessarily an indication of openness, still less of intimacy, or even interest. It is simply one of the formalities of democracy – an informal formality – based on the creed of equality.

It is also, in a way, a means of freeing other people from any kind of bond. The friendliness is an easy gesture of good-will. No demands are made and the other person is set free to get on with his own life and make good. 'The bond of human affections', said de Tocqueville, 'is extended but it is relaxed.' The friendliness, in short, is somehow impersonal. It is imitation intimacy, instant love. In recent years this surface of palliness has been given a high gloss by the great unifying force of American cultural life, commercial TV.

HARDWICK: Those strange sort of sentimental locutions are rather new to America and they're very noticeable if you've been away for a short time. Of course, all this, alas, comes from television, where you find these masters of ceremonies on these endless programmes all calling each other by their first names. The lady, who's never seen this man who makes several hundred thousand dollars a year, says: 'Hello, Bill. No, Bill. Yes, Bill'; and he calls her Jane, though she's fifty or sixty years old. Now, a taxi-driver, who has been complaining all the time and seems to be absolutely wretched, when you get out he says: 'Have a pleasant day' – which is pure TV language. But somehow he feels more real saying that than if he said nothing, because it's this sort of new language.

A.A.: The essence of this new language is, I think, a constant, urgent grasping at cosiness.

HARDWICK: The whole language of America has deteriorated or changed under TV and it is true people think they feel like the slogans rather than otherwise. I noticed in my own child – she's very young, else I wouldn't record it for posterity about her – she told me that a friend of hers, a little boy, had said that he didn't believe in God; that it was all nature and there was no God. And she said to me: 'How can anybody not believe in a great personality like God?' And so you do find even children thinking in these terms which come to them through advertisements really. One of the things that's so marvellous about the film *Dr Strangelove* is that it captures to the most perfect extent, without falsifying, this wonderful inability of Americans, especially those under fifty, to think in any way except in these slogans.

A.A.: The reliance on clichés takes strange forms and permeates unexpected places.

KEMPTON: We had an extraordinary experience in the United States: a month after Mr Kennedy died, President Johnson delivered a eulogy on the steps of the Lincoln Memorial to a large crowd of people which was a pastiche of Lincoln's second Inaugural address. I don't know anything about what things were like in 1860, but it is very hard for me to imagine Andrew Jackson getting up and delivering a eulogy for Abraham Lincoln which was lifted *with pride* from Washington's farewell address.

A.A.: This question of using the acceptable language or appropriate cliché comes up on all levels. For example, when I was discussing the possibilities of an American national health scheme with Dr George Silver, a professor of social medicine, he remarked:

SILVER: You know the story of Professor Thomas McKeown's I told you: the two political parties are like two bottles of medicine which are identical but have different labels. As far as the possibility of getting any effective legislation is concerned, they both practise a form of political contraception, in which no matter how suggestive the preliminary movements, there are no embarrassing legislative consequences. It certainly goes for health; there isn't going to be any effective health legislation.

A.A.: Maybe, but I got the distinct impression that some form of national health scheme may well emerge, provided the correct language is used. That is, provided those who are trying to promulgate the idea don't refer to it as 'socialized medicine' – with all the taboo political overtones that phrase has – but call it, as Kennedy did, 'medicare', which has all the acceptable overtones of a commercial brand name.

But none of this explains why so many Americans in their ordinary casual conversation seem to aspire to the cooing, crooning note of the good, soft-sell advertisement. Part of it, no doubt, is a habit of mind induced by so much television. The less original and educated, when they want to express feelings, slip automatically into the clichés with which they have been provided. Where the advertisers are trying to sell a line of goods, they are trying, however obscurely, to sell – to themselves or to others – the American way of life.

HARDWICK : One thing I feel is important about America, though, and very real, is this sentimental feeling about the country. That's one of the deepest things in American psychology. They really do feel that this is the best country in the world for anyone to live in. And a lot of that is justified and corroborated by the large numbers of foreigners who do want to live in America. And I think that on an existential level it makes a certain amount of sense. The people really feel this. The war made them contrast America with other countries. They've always contrasted it a little bit with South America, and now with certain islands, like Puerto Rico and so on. They take very deeply into their pores the fact that these millions of Puerto Ricans, who might be in the sun, want to come and live in the slums of New York. This is terribly important. When you go to Texas and California and the middle of America, that feeling of well-being by comparison with the rest of the world, that even a very simple person has, is one of the things that's so complicated about America. You can't say it's false.

A.A. : But at a deeper level this tendency to use language for a kind of commercialization of feeling is so strong because it is so soothing. It is as though private life were made less sharp by being talked of in exclusively public language. Clichés provide an immunization against personal pain and confusion, and also against that continual sense of violence and extremity which runs under even the most comfortable American life. After all, language is not the only tranquillizer they use.

HOWE : The main trend in the dominant sections of the middle class in America is towards adjustment, towards finding ways of getting by and getting along. I don't mean anything necessarily very harsh or moralistic in making this description. I think there is, beneath the society, tremendous explosive force. The explosive force consists in various marginal groupings: Negroes, the young, homosexuals,

151

various other people who don't fit into the genteel pattern on the surface. But, in any case, there is a tendency in the middle class towards this kind of adjustment. One form of it is a great stress upon psycho-analysis: you go to your analyst to be smoothed down, to be eased off, to be rounded out, not so that you will live up to the image of yourself, which is being frustrated in your social life, but rather that you will abandon that image of yourself and learn to conform to the images which society imposes upon you. And in that sense, it may be said that psycho-analysis makes for unhappiness, even if also, at times, for contentment.

ZERO MOSTEL: The man had a terrible problem because he had a thirty-thousand-dollar home and could afford to send his boy to college. There was this awful problem, some kind of internal, mental problem that didn't mean anything. So it's like the fellow goes to analysis and he's cured completely. He's so cured that he comes out and the world is still a nuthouse.

A.A.: The nuthouse of modern America is made up of paradoxes, basically that of the immense possibilities of good – comfort, liberalism, decent living, good-will, and equality – offset by an equally immense potentiality for destruction: the assassination of Kennedy, the prejudice, the indifference, the mechanical inhumanity and, most of all, the continual undertone of violence and racial antagonism. They are paradoxes which are not resolvable. And beyond them is a genuine anxiety about the very modernity of the surface of American life. The discrepancy between the beautifully tailored machines and smooth organization, and the painful, trivial inefficiency of ordinary life is so great that it's easy to believe that the expression of ordinary human feelings can scarcely straddle it. That is the basic problem for the artists, and it will be the subject of the last of these programmes [Chapter 7]. For the rest, it is perhaps easier to use the feelings that are provided by the machine itself: that is, the tranquillizing, amiable platitudes of advertising. The gap may be enormous, but life, after all, must go on.

HARDWICK: There's someone – I think it was an English person, I'm not sure – said in conversation that the American ideal is: 'Take up your cross and relax.'

7. The Problems of the Artist

In this series of broadcasts on America – as in those on the Communist countries which preceded it – I have been trying to define the different kinds of pressure brought to bear on the artists and intellectuals, the pressures which make them choose certain means of expression and certain subjects rather than others.

No one, I imagine, would deny that the artists are more acutely aware than most of the pressure on them of society, or reality – or whatever you wish to call it. Without that awareness and the ability to use it for their own ends, they would either sink themselves into the system, as, say, many of the white- and blue-collared workers do, and allow it to shape their identities; or, like politicians and big businessmen, they would try to ride the system, use it, shape it perhaps, and certainly milk it for their own good. The artist, however, suffers from an exacerbated consciousness of both his identity and his society. He is easy with neither; they nag at him. So his art is an attempt to make this discomfort less acute, or to give it at least some coherence of its own by informing it with his insights. R. P. Blackmur defines the problem this way:

BLACKMUR: Somehow or other one either is or is not brought up with the notion that one must press out of oneself what one can press. In Pascal, there is an observation that we are constantly putting obstacles at the edge of the precipice so that we will not fall in. Perhaps you could put it that, in philosophy, the West has largely been concerned for the last three hundred and fifty years with a malicious criticism of knowledge, so that you should come out with a grand and beautiful uncertainty as to the very knowledge upon which you are practising every moment. So in the arts it would seem to be a kind of movement whereby you had a malicious criticism of all those immediate values which you persistently enjoy, and without which you would be lost.

A.A.: In order to define or criticize, however maliciously or benevolently, you need some kind of framework of values, some kind of cipher by which to decode and interpret your dis-ease. In the very broadest and most simple-minded terms, my theory behind these *Under Pressure* broadcasts has been that east of Berlin, this framework is provided by Marx, west of Berlin by Freud. (This, I repeat, is a gross simplification.) In Eastern Europe, the artist, whether explicitly political in his thinking or not, tends to externalize his pressure and translate it into terms of society, whereas in the West, he internalizes it and translates society in terms of his own identity. Even when he is most exacerbatingly aware of the society around him and the pressures it is exerting on him and his actions, he takes them all into himself; he sees social uneasiness as a reflection of his own inner disturbances.

This stress on the isolated individual is very much part of the American tradition. You can see it, to give a couple of trivial examples, in two of their popular myths: that of the log-cabin to White House and that of the Western. The first is the myth of individual achievement against the odds, against accidents, against obstacles, but not fundamentally against society. (Compare, for instance, the rise and fall of Julien Sorel, the hero of Stendhal's *Le Rouge et le Noir*. He climbs the social ladder and triumphs over society; but when he finally falls and is, by accident almost, condemned to death, it is, as he himself says, the hierarchical social order that has reasserted itself. And this is a basically un-American activity or perception.) As for the Western: in it the concept of impartial and accepted law is, as it were, de-socialized. That is, it is reduced to a question of individual courage and morality. The law wins because a man is strong, fast on the draw, and – despite all seductions – just. In Europe, on the other hand, the law is the law.

It is a generally accepted code, not an individual achievement. More or less.

It is, then, part of the American democratic tradition for each individual to assume isolated responsibility for himself. Yet this existential-seeming position has its causes in the structure of American society, as de Tocqueville pointed out:

> As each class approximates to other classes, and intermingles with them, its members become indifferent, and as strangers to one another. Aristocracy had made a chain of all the members of the community, from the peasant to the king: democracy breaks that chain, and severs every link of it . . . [Its citizens] are nothing to any man, they expect nothing from any man; they acquire the habit of always considering themselves as standing alone and they are apt to imagine that their whole destiny is in their own hands.
>
> Thus not only does democracy make every man forget his own ancestors, but it hides his descendants and separates his contemporaries from him; it throws him back for ever upon himself alone, and threatens in the end to confine him entirely within the solitude of his own heart.

In the hundred and thirty-odd years since then this democratic isolation has increased as the social basis for it has become more extreme. To the visitor, modern America sometimes seems like some elaborate conjuring trick: a flourishing, complicated, more-or-less stable society, based on total instability. Everything seems to be in flux; mobility is the rule. People are always on the move. Not only do they travel endlessly and without hesitation, they are also constantly uprooting their homes. After the emigrations, come the migrations; a surprisingly large proportion of the population flows restlessly from one city to another every year. And this mobility extends to everything: to possessions, for instance; the economy booms because products are continually being bought and discarded, buildings put up and torn down again, and so on. Even personal relationships are mobile: the divorce rate is staggering; nothing is for keeps.

SCHLESINGER: Mobility has been historically the character of American life from the very beginning. It is a country settled by people who came from other countries. The development of the nation is the development of constant movements to the west. Today there is no longer a geographical frontier, but twenty per cent of Americans move from one place to another in the course of every year. This does mean that society has an evanescence, that personal relationships have a discontinuity. This has affected American art and American thought from the beginning. James's pragmatism, his radical empiricism, is an attempt to provide a philosophic expression of the texture, or rather the lack of continuity in the texture of American society. This is a problem with which our artists and our political leaders have had to cope from the very beginning. In a sense, the problem is rendered more intense by the increase in the velocity of society. Everything is lived more intensely, everything is consumed more intensely. Take a simple example: a comedian, who half a century ago could be a success in vaudeville for twenty-five years by repeating one or two or three acts, is now dead after a year in television. This increase in the rate of consumption is a hard thing. But the condition differs only quantitively, not qualitatively, from what it's always been.

A.A.: For the writer, this mobility produces a specific and exhausting form of pressure.

HARDWICK: There is this feeling of speed, that a year must not pass without something to show – a book, or some sort of progress that you can show to the public, and to yourself of course. It might be possible but it's very difficult for me to imagine *Finnegan's Wake* produced in America after the war: the long, long wait in poverty, the uncertainty of the outcome; this absolutely original, difficult work that took – I've forgotten whether it's eleven or fourteen years. It may not be possible for anyone to devote himself that single-mindedly, with that feeling that he is doing something worth while. Again, this speed may in some way be connected with the sense of change – that one can change anything and move on to something new all the time – that is so typical of our society.

A.A.: The novelist, James Baldwin, describes the more persecutory effects of this pressure:

BALDWIN: It is very hard to be an American success. Henry James said it much better than I did; he said that no one could survive being an American success. If you're an American novelist and you look at the record – by which I mean Faulkner, Hemingway, any novelist you can think of – it's a record of exiles. Then you begin to think about what happened really to Fitzgerald, what happened really to Hemingway. Why is it that until today almost no American novelist has outlived his first novel? Why is it that you can be considered in some other country as a writer with a right to his failures, with a right to his experiments, and here you must be a success? No writer writes a book every year, and the pressure you're put under *is* to write a book every year. As they say in Hollywood, you're only as good as your last movie. Well, any artist lives with failure, he does not live with success. Success is not a real word, it's an American word. And if you're a black writer . . . oh, my friend, no matter what they say – what they did for me, how lucky I am – it isn't true. I'm the man behind the typewriter, I have to write the books, I have to deal with it, I have to support my own performance, which I distrust, in a country which thinks it is more important to be a success than it is to be an artist.

A.A.: The pressure, however, is not simply to succeed and make money; it is something which also seems to drive Americans to a kind of psychological improvisation, a constant inner mobility.

KEMPTON: I remember I talked to a Texan about Dallas

and he said that a typical Texan was not born there; the typical Texan was Jack Ruby, for example, who came to Dallas because Dallas called him there. It's quite true that each city gets the immigrants it deserves, but when you talk about mobility, the mobility of American life, it's also true that your fantasies and prejudices are mobile. People are always going to San Francisco from the rest of the world, you know, seeking atmosphere and unfortunately bringing none with themselves. People go to New Orleans in a special way. And the young man from the provinces in the United States has all sorts of capital cities to go to. Dallas is one of these capital cities, New York is another, San Francisco is another, New Orleans is another. So you do have this intense kind of moving about. But it is the business of so much American life, I think, so much of the American rise and change being an obliteration of your own background. It is terribly hard with Americans, as we get less and less regional, to imagine what a man's father was like. I used to say that some of the way you got up in the world was parricide. Well, to a certain extent we forgive parricide in the United States overwhelmingly. This is why we go in for Freudianism more than almost any other country. Automatically, the Process, the Trial, is the judgement of the parent by the child. The psychiatrist has replaced the priest. Now, whatever you say about the priest, he represents a continual tradition which you can engage in love or hate. The psychiatrist represents a century which is attempting to abolish all centuries but its own. That is, the American psychiatrists; not Freud, but the American psychiatrist represents this. This is the how-to cult, the how-to-live. No one's ever written how-to-feel, how-to-love, any of these books. We don't write those because we're scared of them.

A.A. : Once upon a time, people emigrated to the States in search of a better life, or a possible life, or just a life. Nowadays America's internal migrants are in search of their own identities. The general mobility has become a symbol of a kind of inner disability. Witness our most distinguished export poet, who has lived in the States for the last twenty-five years and now totes an American passport:

w. h. auden: One thing that does seem to me different, compared with what I knew in England when I was young, that is the fluidity of society in this country. The change in the way you live, even the income you have, means that you can no longer answer the question 'Who am I?' by saying, as one used to be able to, 'Well, I'm a member of such and such a family, such and such a class' and so on, which then, of course, you can refine down and say 'Well, I'm not exactly the same as my parents, I'm not exactly identical with the middle class', or whatever the class is. But here, people seem to have to answer the question 'Who am I?' straight away, in personal terms, which I believe is very difficult to do. And I suspect that is a great strain for them.

I think intellectuals here lack the sense of belonging to a class. I mean to the clerisy or whatever you like to call it. They do sort of feel that the whole cultural burden of the country falls on their shoulders, which nobody in Europe does. You think of yourself as a member of a whole class of people descended presumably from medieval clergy of whom you're one member, and that what *you* can't do, somebody else can do. Here, I think people do think: 'Well, everything falls on me.'

a.a.: This responsibility of the artist to himself, the feeling that he has to create his whole world – his moral order, his style and his tradition – for himself and from scratch, seems to be a belief shared by almost every American writer I've ever met.

ellison: Our problem, of course, is one of individuals. Auden defines a democracy as a collectivity of individuals. And that's one of the main problems: the individual does confront, or at least he's put in the position of confronting events. He only acts responsibly when he tries to think about the meaning of events and their importance to himself and to the nation, and then he renders a judgement. That's what makes being an American so difficult. It's true every individual is in a position of judging, but the difference here is that much hangs upon his judgement. It can't be discharged through the functioning of a government really, or through a class or through a party. What the individual does in relationship to events, to issues, really falls back upon his own conscience and his own consciousness. He realizes himself as an American precisely through taking on individual responsibility. Well, of course, with the writer, with the artist, with the intellectual this presses in very hard.

GOLD: The magnifying glass that the American writer tends to use is himself, almost without reference to the outside world. But if he's any good at all, the outside world is refracted through him. He doesn't have a theory. He has his energy, or his lasciviousness, or his desire to make a personal focus. It forces a high development of style in the best writers. He doesn't have a theory to lean on, so therefore he has to find only his personal voice. The American writer is a little in the position of a cock on a dung-heap. He surveys the whole world with rather dirty feet. If he has joy, if he's capable of joy, it's the product of his own ability to assimilate a lot of elements which would revolt other people. A writer is often a man who cures himself of suicide, or cures himself of terrible pessimism by the act of expression. It's, I think, a paradox that many of the best writers, in a very bad time, are filled with fun and humour – not even with satire, but with just pure *joie de vivre*.

A.A.: Whether or not art can be useful as a kind of psychotherapy is, for the moment, slightly beside the main point – which is that the writer has only himself both to blame and also to refer to. If he has a framework, he

F
161

creates it himself out of himself, without much help from society. If Murray Kempton is right and the general American public runs for reassurance to the psychiatrist and the how-to books – all those how-to-win-friends-and-influence-people, how-to-succeed-in-business-without-really-trying, how-to-service-your-own-Volkswagen, and how-to-achieve-nirvana books – the writers, in contrast, are using their art as their own personal how-to: how to have an identity.

ELLISON: You pick and choose and you make yourself. This is one of the freedoms in the United States and one that we all find very, very troublesome. We are obligated to create ourselves, not as a matter of escaping any given background but of enriching it.

A.A.: This, too, is nothing new. It is, indeed, part of the American tradition:

HOWE: The very best American writers always are involved in defining the terms of their own existence. This often means defining the terms of their own rebellion. This goes all the way back to Melville. In fact, Melville is the patron saint of this kind of activity. And in doing this, they set themselves up as sort of isolate rebels against society, often with great dignity and honour, and you might even say glory. By contrast, reading certain English writers from a distance, what strikes me is that for them the modes of expression are – to some extent – given, available, ready. This makes for economy, I think, but sometimes of course it makes for a certain conventionality.

A.A.: To take Melville as the patron saint of modern American literature helps make sense of the whole complexity. This democratic need to quarrel with God and to define yourself in terms of a totally original art-form – quite new and quite different for each artist – makes for the peculiar intensity of American writing: its ambitiousness, energy, obsessive originality (which often means resorting to mannerism to achieve it), and its slightly romantic grandeur, guilt and sense of achievement.

LOWELL: We have some impatience with the sort of prosaic, everyday things of life, that sort of whimsical patience that other countries may have. That's really painful to endure: to be minor and so forth. We leap for the sublime. You might almost say that American literature and culture begin with *Paradise Lost*. I always think there are two great symbolic figures that stand behind American ambition and idealism and culture. One is Milton's Lucifer and the other is Captain Ahab. These two sublime ambitions that are doomed. I suppose this is too apocalyptic to put it this way, but it's the Ahab story of having to murder evil, and you may murder all the good with it if it gets desperate enough to struggle. Now Russia's in somewhat the same position, of course, and it's a world situation now. But it hits our genius in a very strange way. What's best in our country in a way is united with this, and what's worst and most dangerous and naked and inhuman about us gets swept up into this ideal. Also this thing that we won't let go, a kind of energy and power of imagination, of throwing ourselves all out into something.

It's often said we have no minor poets in America, though of course we do. But that seems an oddly ignoble ambition. Even the minor poet reaches for the sublime. What one finds wrong with American culture is the monotony of the sublime. I've never lived anywhere else, but I feel maybe what is extreme and perhaps unique about America is that for the artist his existence becomes his art; he's reborn in it and he hardly exists without it. A friend of mine went to London this summer. He was utterly delighted with it and said, 'It's so human' (he comes from the South). 'Its people were so polite, and it just seemed unimaginably gentle and wonderful in the way an American city isn't.' But he avoided meeting any English literary people. He felt that England was a disaster for the literary man, that he was hampered at every step with cautions and 'nots' and things.

I don't know enough about Englishmen or any other country to make a comparison, but I feel that we have a feeling the arts should be all out. If you're in it, you're all out in it and you're not ashamed to talk about it endlessly and rather sheerly. That would seem embarrassing to an Englishman and inhuman probably, to be that all-out about it. I guess the American finds something uninvigorating about the Englishman in that he doesn't plunge into it. Art is always done with both your hands in America. The artist finds new life in it and almost sheds his other life.

A.A.: Now, this 'all-outness' Lowell talks about can be invigorating. American artists – good, bad, and indifferent – are usually more serious about their work than, say, the English; more willing to stick their necks out with something new, difficult, tentative, and not at all willing to accept a comfortable niche in literary history as a competent minor artist. But it can also be limiting. That is, it can deteriorate into that same obsessive professionalism which comes to any society as massive, compartmentalized and technological as the United States. It makes the artist into just another specialist technician in one form of consumer entertainment. And a good many American artists resent this. For example, when I asked Zero Mostel about his painting, he replied this way:

MOSTEL: The thing that is kind of interesting to me is that you say, 'Oh, you are a painter too.' It's an amazing thing that now we live in such a specialized world. You only do one thing, do half of one thing, but do it well, or a tenth of one thing and do it well, or a fiftieth of one thing and do it well. You can't do two things, three things, four things. There are many hours in a day and you can do many things. But there's a restriction to your freedom of that kind because it requires money to do. Always the root of it is money, economics. I, for instance, I couldn't give up painting, I have to do painting. I know it's like the criminal who says: 'I have a need to kill' but I think it's much more acceptable to drip a little water-colour on a piece of paper than go out gunning down people, you see. There should be that kind of mental attitude that people should try many things, they shouldn't be afraid, they should be exposed to many things, to diverse things, to diverse ideas. You talk about the free market of ideas – there is no free market of ideas. The unions and the whole set-up is to do so many hours of work which tire you, leave you no room for anything else, you understand? If they show you one style of painting, that's all you should take, because the other requires a little more writing, a little more understanding, a little more philosophy, a little more what-have-you in order to have it. So everything is safe. Today you look at a painting, it's drips; if it drips, it's good. The theatre, if there's a little sex in it, if there's a little farce in it, it's good. If its writing, the guy has exposed himself and tells you all about himself and his love affairs, it's good; that will be published. Not too much, don't go any farther afield than that. That's the terrible price you pay for this kind of specialization, both mentally and what you do for your living.

A.A.: Yet Mostel's brand of Renaissance all-roundness is not at all an American thing. What is more usual is a fierce energy channelled in one direction. If it produces what Lowell calls 'a monotony of the sublime' that may be an artistic equivalent of that ambitious sense of democratic possibility which America exudes in its less gloomy and introspective moments, a kind of corollary of the belief that every citizen is, theoretically, able to become President or a millionaire. Every artist feels he has a right to become Melville. W. H. Auden, in a rather English way, disapproves of this ambition:

AUDEN: A thing that always puzzles me in America is a kind of Utopian perfectionism which makes people very unwilling to accept their own personal limitations. I think why so many people go off to analysts is because they think they ought to have a perfect personality. They're not prepared to put up with the one they have.

A.A.: Now the particular emphasis of contemporary American psycho-analysis is scarcely encouraging to artistic creation; that is, it seems less devoted to helping the patient to accept the forces at work in his personality than to adjusting his personality to fit society. And this tendency is fundamentally at odds with all art, however well it may suit mass-society.

KEMPTON: Now, I don't know why we are this way, it's terribly difficult for us to express. It's because we are a social-science people and our intellectuals are social-science intellectuals. The poet is an outsider, not because he's a Bohemian – since American poets tend to be among the most extraordinarily respectable citizens of our society – he is an outsider because the thing he's working on is a dilettante thing. An American magazine, which appeals to intellectual readers and which announces to its advertisers that it appeals to intellectual readers, will say 'Our readers are more intellectual than anybody else's readers because they prefer works of non-fiction to works of fiction'. Now, the position of the novel in the United States is inferior to the position of any work of social science I can think of – that is, the new novel, the unfashionable novel. It is because the novel describes an interior, and works of social science affect to tell you the truth about an exterior that we're more comfortable with. And that's why Americans carry cameras everywhere, because they're afraid to look. And Freud comes to us, you see, and we go to Freud and we listen to our psychiatrist about everything, because we are afraid of our poets and novelists.

A.A.: If I am right about what I called 'the internalization of pressure' in American art, then both the American style of psycho-analytic adjustment and the whole trend towards sociology is flatly against the current of the best American writing. Robert Lowell said that the American artist makes his life out of his art. According to Norman Mailer, he also recreates his society in his own image or in his own head.

MAILER: In America we're always creating and re-creating our picture of the world. Every American is always writing a vast social novel in his head; a social novel in which various people come to power because they've obeyed certain matters and ignored others, were bold at the appropriate moment. The idea of social boldness, after all, also involves secondarily a notion of a structure to society. Since we don't have a clear structure to our society, we're always rewriting in our heads what that possible structure could be. Every American, every ambitious American, no matter what he's doing – he may be a machinist in a small shop in Iowa – but if he is at all ambitious he is rewriting his picture of the world all the time.

A.A.: It stands to reason then that the picture of the world the American artist is trying to create will be a counter-balance to that prefabricated, mass-produced, permissive vision of reality marketed most energetically from 1952 to 1960 by Eisenhower Incorporated. It was labelled the American Way of Life and it came with a companion package: Togetherness.

HOWE: We live in a society now, in America, where moderation has become an absolute positive virtue; no-body except a few people on both extremes dares to challenge it. It has become really the dominant cant phrase of American society. At the same time, it's a society with a very strong tradition of violence behind it, also of personal violence. We had a dismal tragic example of this in the assassination of the President. So the problem becomes: how do you find a way of reconciling the social moderation, the social timidity, the social evasiveness of the world in which we live, with the impulse towards personal extremism, personal violence, personal break-through, or personal neuroses and psychoses? I think the best writers of our time in America – Faulkner and one or two others – coped with this particular problem. But, of course, a problem that can be coped with in literary terms and make for a great work, isn't necessarily thereby solved in terms of actual experience.

A.A.: It is, then, the sense of trouble, which exists despite all the wealth and comfort and niceness, which most concerns American artists now.

LOWELL: I have a feeling that the arts are in a very funny position now; that we are free to say what we want to and somehow what we want to say is the confusion and sadness and incoherence of the human condition. While anyone running a government must say the opposite of that – that it can be solved, it can be run – and must take an optimistic stance. I don't know why the arts say this so strongly. It may be a miserable time, more than others. The world is liable to blow up and we're in some kind of transition domestically – I mean in one's family life and everything else. There are new moral possibilities, new moral inco-herence. It's a very confused moment. And for some reason, it's almost a dogma with us that we'll show that confusion.

A.A.: In some curious way, the confusion and moral incoherence and sense of danger is something that the American public wants to hear about at the moment. Perhaps it's the result of a dim apprehension of the signi-ficance of the bomb, or the race riots, or the assassination of the President. Or perhaps it's simply a matter of fashion and the publicity machine.

ELLISON: I think that very often the public wants to be

made aware of the chaotic aspects of reality. They want this very much, but they want it in such a fashion that they're not going to be too much upset. The Americans have a terrific way of blunting the point or the cutting edge of highly moral art, and you can only hope that whatever you write will last long enough for them to be forced back to it through events.

A.A.: Ellison's own superb novel, *Invisible Man*, which dealt brilliantly with the difficulty of taking the outer chaos into oneself and making sense of it, was published way back in 1947. But I'm not sure that its implications were fully taken at that time. It was successful, but what Ellison calls its 'cutting edge' was blunted when it was hailed as a great *Negro* novel rather than as an artistic and moral achievement. The fashion for chaotic and protesting art began later with a much more trivial but better publicized occasion, the so-called Beat Revolution. According to Norman Mailer, this was the beginning of some kind of new artistic freedom – a freedom which defined itself less in artistic terms than by its antithesis to Madison Avenue's world of advertising, mass persuasion and glossy magazines.

MAILER: I think the reason they gave such a cultural shock is that up to that point Madison Avenue had pretty much been running the cultural life of America. And with a great deal of confidence. Everything they tried worked out pretty much the way they thought it was going to work out. Whenever *Time* magazine, let's say, or *Life* magazine wished to interest Americans in some period, they could just sit around their Board table and say: 'Now, let's have a large series this Fall on the Renaissance. It's about time the American people learnt something about the Renaissance.' There was this virtually dictated set of directions being given to American culture. The Americans were being brought up by mother. So the Beatniks arrived to strain this image altogether. It was a little bit as if father had suddenly come home, weak and out of hospital and dead drunk, but a figure in the household.

It was a tiny revolution, but the result was that there was much more liberty after it. Before, it was hard to say anything at all in this country. I don't mean that there was a totalitarian atmosphere. In a subtle way, we may have more of a totalitarian atmosphere today, although a very benevolent totalitarianism. But at that time, everything was terribly cut and dried, everything was really determined. You knew if you wrote a piece and went up to a certain point you were all right. After that, you were going across a line of no return; there were going to be negative results. Your piece would not be accepted by a magazine, or if it was a novel, you were going to get bad reviews. You could almost measure it to a fine point. You could say: 'If I put this sentence in, the *New York Times Book Review* will not give me the front page for this book.' It was just as clear cut as that.

When the Beatniks came in, they were like a small hand-grenade that went off in the middle of an antique shop. By the time they'd finished sweeping up the crockery, there was a lot of space left on the shelf and the Establishment had to fill it with all sorts of new things. The result is a lot of writers – I won't say came out of that small Beat Revolution, but they have been given liberty by it – like Terence Southern, Joe Heller, and Stanley Kubrick. I don't think *Dr Strangelove* could have been made without that Beat revolution seven years ago. But the interesting aspect of it, the reason it was a revolution, was that Ginsberg dared something which no one in the literary world had dared at all – which is he dared precisely to take the lid off his own jar and show the various jellies and sweetmeats and – dare I say it? – the maggots inside, which offended and horrified and fascinated everyone. We just hadn't had something quite like this in American life perhaps ever; certainly not to that extent.

A.A.: Now, I think Mailer overvalues Ginsberg very considerably. The kind of self-revelation he went in for derived, like his metrical forms, from Walt Whitman. And as Whitman ended up by becoming, rather self-consciously, what the critic Joseph Frank calls 'a propagandist of the American dream', so Ginsberg with his poetry of the analyst's couch is very much at one with modern American platitudes and fads.

Yet if the Beats didn't make it artistically – because of the incurably adolescent quality of their protest – they were well enough publicized to have had an obscure psychic effect on the American public. There is now a taste for artforms which do, one way or another, seem to reflect something of the chaos of American life: the clashing paradoxes of the massified society and the uncomfortable individual; the indignant protest which is so promptly and overwhelmingly rewarded; the vast wealth and intense poverty; the enlightened creed of equality and the appalling racial hatreds; the palliness and the isolation; the counterpoised possibilities of the good life and total destruction; and so on. In short, all those paradoxes I tried to define in the second of these American programmes.

The effect on the arts is that suitably chaotic and paradoxical forms have been evolved with new strength. For example, Lowell's poetry, which is at once highly formal yet intensely and personally disturbed; Saul Bellow's comic tragic novels; or a film like *Dr Strangelove*, which makes farce out of annihilation (and it's a sure sign of the hold the new forms and tone have taken when they appear in an interpretative art like the commercial cinema, which is rarely, in any real sense, in the *avant-garde*).

How, then, would the writers define the contemporary modes?

GOLD : The contemporary American style almost has to be comic style, by which I obviously don't mean un-serious. Well, to think of writers that I know – many of them have jobs other than writing and they're all comic jobs: speculating in the Stock Market, driving a cab; no writers have serious jobs. Teaching, for example – another comic job. The serious jobs don't earn enough living.

To talk about comedy is not to say that there's necessarily happiness to go with it. There's a motto that Camus quotes in his journals, which comes to mind. I've a very bad memory, but it's something like: 'What bars our way, increases our need to travel along that way.' The fact that so much contemporary life is not a happy occasion obliges writers, in order to control their experience, to make jokes about it.

ELLISON: The madness, the humour arises out of the sense that, in the United States, one mode will turn into the other, tragedy will turn into comedy, comedy will turn into tragedy, because in the centre of all this is not God in the old sense, but man himself, man's inability to really define a situation and control it. You can project a pattern, you can make a constitution, but inevitably there is a clash between your desires and your ideals, between your ideals and your conduct. This leads to a sense of the ironic, and a sense of the comic. Of course part of this, when it comes from people of minority backgrounds, is the blending of the minority humour. I'm sure that Bellow gets a lot of the Yiddish irony into his work because he comes out of a people whose source of humour has expressed an ironic view. And the same is true for Negroes. Quite a lot of the nonsense quality of American popular humour goes back to Negroes and this goes back to slavery and back to the absurd predicament of Negroes. I'm not talking of French existentialism. I'm talking about being part of a country where everyone else was free and you were not free. But you were free enough to observe to what extent they were not free.

Certainly slavery in a great democratic country was very absurd indeed. So you've got this, this underground quality, you've got the sense of reality which underlies appearances. Now they're talking about under-classes in this country. Well, there is an under-humour, and the under-humour, I think, expresses reality at its most chaotic. If there's a certain heroism in it, it lies in the fact that you can conceive of so much chaos without being destroyed. And this is what you get in much of the work by American writers at the moment, certainly in the novelists; at least, this is what they're trying to deal with.

A.A.: Granted this new 'underground' art connects with the under classes and also with the violent under-forces of American society. But it is also very much, as Ellison says, a product of minority groups, particularly of the Jews. Indeed, it is extraordinary the degree to which nearly everything we think of as most representative of contemporary American culture – as it is manifested in books and movies and paintings, all export images – is in fact either created by American Jews or deeply influenced by them: the whole of the intellectual life and the entertainment world for example, much of the creative writing and even the food.

LOWELL: I think there wouldn't be any active American culture now without the Jewish element. They are small in numbers, but they're a leaven that changes the whole intellectual world of America. It's a painful reality that a minority should have such liveliness and vigour. You're sort of at a loss why the rest of the country doesn't equal that.

HARDWICK: You feel that when you leave New York you can't find anyone that knows what you're talking about, because you run into real Americans, as they're called – as they call themselves – from other places. It's very difficult to communicate with them. One of the things about America that strikes me at least is that when you go to small towns, inasmuch as there are any small towns that have any character left, you feel you've gone to a foreign country, because there are no Jews there. And the whole sort of Jewish note that's in fiction and in popular culture is the most important thing. I don't know quite how to analyse how it came about, but it's very real.

A.A. : Perhaps the Jewish influence is so strong because of the depth to which American life has become urbanized; and the Jews are a dominantly urban race. Equally, it is in the cities where the chaotic paradoxes are most powerful and most evident.

HARDWICK : I think this urban aspect of present-day fiction is very strong, yet it's terribly difficult even to absorb the city. And that's why I would say in the last fifteen years, Jewish fiction has taken the place of Southern fiction which was the best before, coming out of small towns and stable relationships and comic figures, and racial contrast, social contrast. Well, now that seems to have died out as the small town has somewhat been absorbed, and as people in the most remote little place in Alabama now all look at television and say the same things and feel the same things – except that in the South they hate the Negro more. That's about all that's left of these regional differences which have been absolutely absorbed since the war. Well now, the Jewish fiction, which is the fiction of the city, since the war has been – at least to my mind – much the most important American fiction.

A.A. : Yet one of the curiosities of contemporary American literature is a kind of ethnic split between poetry and the novel. The really important poets, I mean, are all non-Jews: Lowell, Berryman, Roethke, Sylvia Plath; whilst the important novelists, since the generation of Faulkner and Hemingway, are nearly all Jews or Negroes: Bellow, Mailer, Heller, Baldwin, Ellison. (There are, of course, plenty of exceptions on both sides, but none important enough, I think, to disprove the rule.) I put this to the critic, Mark Schorer:

SCHORER : It's an interesting point. After all, the novel

has to come out of social relationships. Most social relationships for non-Jewish, non-minority groups of any kind are no longer meaningfully existent in the United States. There are business relationships but they're not meaningful; they're all kinds but they don't somehow relate to a community. The Jewish writer has the advantage of being able to identify himself with a community; even the Negro writer can do that, objecting as he may to that very identification. And this is, after all, the source of the material for fiction. Poetry can come out of the subjective life of the individual and it can be completely divorced from any community, right? I was thinking of a novelist like Bernard Malamud who can take off from the manners of a Jewish block, let us say, in a metropolitan centre and then, from that base, handle great, important, universal things. And this is not the privilege of people who have no such localized cultural inheritance. After all, the history of America is the history of improvisation, of new people coming to a new place, having to play everything by ear, the situation unfamiliar, their institutions impossible to transfer. So we began with a kind of continual shifting of what the first settlers brought with them, which means that nothing was ever settled. In the meantime, other groups came into the United States and maintained, up to a point, their cultural traditions as well as they could, and religious groups could maintain them with a certain consistency. The Jewish writers in fiction came from under-privileged Jewish groups within an industrial society, not privileged Jewish groups; and the under-privileged Jews maintained their own inheritance in a way that probably the privileged Jew does not.

A.A.: It's important, however, to make less of the limitations of a Jewish background for a writer than of the possibilities it opens up.

HARDWICK: Some people have suggested that Jewish fiction is another form of regionalism, but the most important Jewish fiction is not that way. It's not Momma's biscuits and Grandfather up in the Bronx. It's this spirit of international rationalism in the face of the real despair and chaos of American life, of bringing some broader spirit to bear on it than the simple recording of regional or local standards. And that's the most important thing about Jewish fiction, I think. That it does come out of some broader, old libertarian, humane, somewhat European tradition.

A.A. : It is a question, then, not of minority quirks but of a larger cultural tradition, a question of aides to the understanding of both the chaotic reality the writer is faced with and his own emergent and probably equally chaotic identity.

HARDWICK : Saul Bellow is particularly interesting in that he is one of the few fiction writers who uses his full intelligence in his fiction. He's one of the most intelligent people in America, I'm sure, if one can think of something like that. But it's very relevant to his work, and he uses every possible aspect of American life; whereas one finds that so many fiction writers are rather afraid of the total thing. They cherish their fears and their limitations, I think, out of fear they won't be able to write anything at all, facing this weird chaos of American life:

A.A. : Saul Bellow himself, however, is strongly opposed to any attempts to romanticize the artist's predicament.

BELLOW : It may be partly the fault of the artist himself in his notion of what he is and what he's doing. He's inherited a romantic tradition which forces him into the position of nay-sayer and Promethean or undergroundling or destroyer of himself, or any number of roles that he feels absolutely obliged to play out. This, it seems to me, is a rather unfortunate thing and probably the result of some misunderstanding. It's hard to blame people for not overcoming personally such a mass of historical trouble which has been cast upon them. But on the other hand, the romantic tradition makes us stress, in our age, the horrors of our situation, the degradation of mankind and makes us paste all sorts of post-Christian, post-Copernican labels all over ourselves, which may or may not be relevant.

A.A.: Bellow is objecting, I suppose, to the slightly modish existential nihilism which prevails in American *avant-garde* writing. Yet the tradition of romantic, rebellious isolation descends at least from Melville. And Melville, presumably, was only able to do what he did because his genius was somehow relevant to the American situation; that is, to the democratic belief in isolated individual responsibility, the desire to create one's self in isolation, to will the self into a certain chosen shape – as the American constitution was in itself a willed intellectual pattern and American civilization was a willed imposing of modern urban life on the chaotic wilderness of an untouched continent. This also touches the Jewish genius very deeply. In Europe the Jews have always been a more-or-less isolated group within the community – however centrally they have been involved in the culture. In the States, on the other hand, they are one of the most dominant elements in the society as a whole. Therefore, the artists among them tend, I think, to carry over into their private work that sense of alienation which is no longer socially justified.

But the present difficulty lies in the degree to which the willed self-creation has been put into reverse and become self-destruction:

BELLOW: I don't really know that it is a question of the individual artist pitted against the situation, the total situation. I think that's rather too ambitious and makes life impossible for the individual and leads him to self-destruction. A certain amount of self-destruction we must undergo, I suppose, to destroy former falsehoods and burn ourselves clean. I don't believe in a kind of apocalypse that calls for the demolition and knocking down of everything that stood before.

A.A. : It seems to me that the self-destructive extremism of so much contemporary American art is the direct result of what I've called the internalization of pressure. The artist, I mean, is working out in the microcosm of his self, the potentialities for destruction which, as we are always being told, surround him everywhere in a nuclear age. But at the same time, the destructiveness is used, paradoxically, to create art. For the artist violence is, therefore, a kind of rhetoric of the time, a means of coping with the American uncertainties.

ELLISON : There is this loneliness which makes for psychological violence, the unknown quality of the country – and there's still an unknown quality of the country. One of the problems arising out of great mobility is that you never know what a place is going to be like five years after you leave it, or maybe only a year after you leave it. And this makes for tension. But I think something else is active here. In order to break through all of the hiked-up commercials, the hiked-up television programmes, and so on, I think the artist feels the need for a greater tension in his work, so that he can somehow approach the reader. This violence to a large extent, then, is rhetorical. Violence must be contained certainly by the artist and it seems to me that he's obligated to get it into his work. If he can't get it into his work, then he becomes an entertainer. He begins to act this thing out before the public. He'll find himself in the position of a man like Charlie Parker, the jazz musician, whose pain, whose ills became part of the attraction. People used to go to see him and as he said: 'I no longer know whether they're coming to hear a musician or to see the greatest junkie in the world, or the supreme hipster.'

A.A. : The difficulty, then, is to assimilate the social violence, mobility, chaos and uncertainty into yourself and yet keep it in control; to use it as a means to art, and not to let it use you; to create, in short, not to compete with Madison Avenue.

ELLISON : I know that many of my friends who are writers of great influence and talent, although they're not wealthy, are people who reject the type of professionalism which would make them victims of their craft. They try to maintain an amateur's freshness of approach and they just turn down a lot of opportunities to make money, not out of any nobility really but out of a desire to protect themselves, to protect that which is most meaningful to them. I feel this way myself. Not only do I write rather slowly, but at a certain point you realize that it's easier to make a million dollars than to write a good novel. So, since you're obviously not going to make a million dollars, you might as well go on and try to write a good novel.

A.A. : No doubt the situation of the writer in America has always been difficult, his responsibilities always enormous. But they are even more extreme now because everything seems to be turning in on him at once. The mass society in which he lives is becoming even more massive, more monolithic, devious, and even more anxious to swallow him up whole. At the same time, the under-forces he can sense at work are more violent, more destructive, and more impossible to contain or deny. And the certainties have become fewer: practically none of the artists profess any religion and, since the thirties, the political alternatives to religion have lost their power; there is, effectively, no viable left-wing ideology in the States. Even the dominant creed of modern America, that of psycho-analysis, helps only to thrust the artist more deeply in on himself. So he is left alone to play out by ear his art, his identity, and even his society on the page in front of him.

BALDWIN : I said it was terrible to be an American success. I mean that, after all, on one fine morning, no matter how I play it, I've got to sit down in front of that typewriter and face a page on which there is nothing written yet. It begins at page one, may end at page seven hundred. When it ends at page seven hundred, you've gone through a voyage and you're not the same person you were when you typed page one.

8. Epilogue: America and Extremist Art

No one imagines that what Elizabeth Hardwick calls 'the weird chaos of American life' can ever be summarized, nor its endless contradictions and paradoxes resolved. Nothing so grandiose: the problem is to define somehow the stir and excitement and tension of the place, its curious mixture of anxiety and over-confidence, violence and apathy, glimmer and filth. Clearly, whatever it is you are looking for you can find. And the foreigner, his view coloured and shifted by those three thousand miles of ocean, is looking for something that probably doesn't much concern the Americans themselves. You come to the States, as Lawrence said, to get away. Travel may or may not broaden the mind, it certainly unbinds the fantasies. So part of your reactions are qualified by that sudden access of emotional freedom that comes when you simply clear out.

With partiality, then, and a great deal of projection, I find the seductiveness of the States in its combination of three ambiguous virtues: loneliness, energy, and independence.

Loneliness. It is a continual, almost palpable quality which the country gives off like a heat shimmer. It is no less present in the utter separateness and indifference of city life, the blank size of the buildings, the self-sufficiency of the different ethnic ghettoes, than in the deserts and mountains of the south-west. It is not made for an instant less by that terrible friendliness, mass-produced, pre-packaged, frozen, that coos at you from every TV screen and billboard. Rather, this false cosiness – instant Doris Day – accentuates the loneliness precisely because it is mass-produced, a convention as chilling and formal as diplomatic protocol. Perhaps it is this style of friendliness without human sympathy that helps to make the Americans so wary of any organized social welfare: in a certain light – that, perhaps, cast by a million television screens – social benevolence looks much like contempt.

Energy. This, too, is part of the physical presence of the country, an aspect of its power, wealth and drive to excel. When Robert Lowell calls American society 'sheer' and Norman Mailer calls it 'totalitarian' both are referring to those monster organizations that seem to control, though often in a benign, soft-selling way, so much of American life. Yet they are also referring to something more subtle and pervasive, something that has perhaps more to do with the probing, dramatic architecture by which the Corporations create one aspect of their public image. It is the same quality as appears in the passionate self-absorption of private life, the unwavering drive to do what you must flat out. There is a continual, impatient nerviness about people, which has less to do with passion than exacerbation. It is at one with that sense of violence which, as Norman Podhoretz says, 'trembles so constantly and ubiquitously below the surface of the life we lead'. It's also at one with the continual tension of intelligence which controls the tone of the best American arts, an unrelaxing energy of the imagination and intellect. This may at times seem battering, bull-headed and – for the arts – paradoxically insensitive. Lowell, with some irritation, calls it 'a monotony of the sublime'. It strikes me as preferable to the Englishman's habitually wan caution and cult of the amateur.

Independence. In a way, this is a combination of the controlling loneliness and energy of American life, which in turn have a cause-and-effect relationship: the energy is released because people essentially leave each other alone to get on with their own isolated lives; there is great envy, greater competitiveness, but peculiarly little interference. American life seems run by a principle of psychic segregation – though not so much separate and equal as separate and driven. This touches some nerve in that American tradition of independence which began with the Declaration and is embodied in the whole concept of democratic equality and in the doctrines of individual grace, salvation, revelation. It is present more potently still in the non-idealistic thrust of successive generations of immigrants seeking the worldly salvation of a successful new life in a successful new country. And this, as Murray Kempton suggests, means 'parricide', the utter obliteration of all background and tradition. Tradition, it is implied, begins now and with us. In the arts, Harold Rosenberg has called this 'the tradition of the new'; another title would be the tradition of traditionlessness. Nothing can be assured; each newcomer of power and ambition feels he has to re-invent his art for himself from scratch, endowing it with his own forms, conventions, language and metaphysics. It is fundamentally a matter of inventing himself, endowing himself with an identity; it also involves, in one degree or another, re-inventing his own society.

This brand of care and attention for the inner life is a luxury product, a result of the material ease and relative wealth of the American intelligentsia. In a country like Poland you can more or less ignore your private troubles because the environment itself is so drably and inescapably in need. In the States, on the other hand, all that comfort exaggerates the personal unease, making it seem gratuitous, intolerable. To the outsider the well-fed, well-paid, endowed and indulged lives of the American intellectuals make their obsessive 'alienation' seem merely a hallucination. Yet, since these are serious men, the concept obviously has some existential reality; it describes sharply enough how they feel towards their environment. It also, as I have suggested, describes a social, almost geographic condition which came long before any fashionable existential theory.

The tradition of traditionlessness lays American artists open to the constant pressure of inner mobility and psychological improvisation, parallel to the constantly shifting, improvised patterns of American society itself. And it is this need continually to play their lives out by ear that makes their work so vital, their influence so central. Nowadays the European intelligentsia turns to the United

States in the same way as, for a long period, they once turned to France: not just for the stimulus of an exploding culture – new ideas, new styles, new fashions – but because they sense under all that turmoil and chic the stirrings of a genuinely advanced sensibility. American artists, that is, seem involved in exploring and defining areas of experience which have not previously been expressed in the arts. Which is, perhaps, no more than a high-pitched way of saying that something moving and unprecedented is happening there.

This advance has been pasted over, like some battered old suitcase, with any number of labels. But the most misleading of them was 'classicism'. Compared with the entranced nineties and tweedy Georgians, Hulme's theories and Eliot's practice may have seemed classical enough in their restraint and intelligence. But in every other way the modern arts are simply a fresh extension of the Romantic movement, the original impulse of which had faded away in moods, atmospherics and generalities. Romanticism in its beginnings had been in the party of revolution, progress and independence, an offshoot of radical politics, a revolt against the assured Augustan pieties of good sense, order, and the deliberate limitation of feelings and language. In place of that the Romantics put the single feeling man in all his oddness and spontaneity. By the beginning of the First World War, Romantic Man, like Augustan Man, had vanished again into the mists of conventionalized high feeling. The modern movement was an attempt to restore him in the light of new realities. First among these was the science of the inner life. Freud once said that 'the poets and philosophers before me discovered the unconscious. What I discovered was the scientific method by which the unconscious can be studied.' From this Lionel Trilling concluded that 'Psycho-analysis is one of the culminations of the Romanticist literature of the nineteenth century'. The hero of modern literature, grandchild of the nineteenth century, is Romantic Man in psychoanalysis.

The difference between classicism and romanticism is

one of province, a difference between the inner and outer worlds. But the difference between the Romantic and the Modern is one of attitude, method and awareness. The Modern is committed not simply to feeling but to thinking about feeling; his attitude is tense, analytic, probing, skilful, dissatisfied. He is concerned not simply with his responses but with the sources of those responses; he is concerned with motives, as in some continually unrolling drama of the self, a drama with no plot, an infinity of reasons, and only one character.

> 'I'll be judge, I'll be jury,'
> Said cunning old Fury

And the fury becomes more cunning, more judging and more furious as the drama progresses.

The movement of the modern arts has been to press deeper and deeper into the subterranean world of psychic isolation, to live out in the arts the personal extremism of breakdown, paranoia and depression. Lawrence once wrote, 'One sheds one's sicknesses in books – repeats and presents one's emotions to be master of them.' This is no longer quite true. The modern artist seems more often to create his sickness in his work, giving himself over to it for the sake of the range and intensity of his art. He cultivates not his own garden but his psychosis or, at the very least, his psychopathic tendencies.

All this has an odd side effect: the complete internalization of all phenomena. Where the Romantics made nature the object of their radical aesthetic politics and the freedom to respond – to nightingale, skylark, daffodils, and the rest – seem like a revolutionary principle, the Moderns seem utterly unaware of the world outside. They live in and on internal landscapes which they may or may not project on to the outer world as seems convenient. As geographers of the underworld and historians of the inner migrations they are always meticulous and preoccupied, often passionate, imaginative, even brave. They have endowed that tangled, badly lit country with a separate and curiously objective life of its own. But in the poetry of, say, Robert Lowell or Sylvia Plath this extraordinary self-awareness is delicately counterbalanced by an utter indifference; the outer world only seems to exist in as much as it can be assimilated. Even an Englishman like Ted Hughes, who starts out as a nature poet and whose work contains more animals than the London Zoo, lavishes all that loving, sharp detail on his menagerie only for whatever corresponding sense of unpredictable violence he finds in himself. He writes like a nature poet gone blind; and he is typical.

The reason for all this is one of the great clichés of our time: the artist is thrown increasingly in on himself by the sheer size and engulfing blankness of industrial society; as life becomes more mass produced, mass organized and statistical the arts become – proportionately, despairingly – more extreme and solipsistic. To this is added the second great cliché: that the crisis situation – the inheritance of the concentration camps, the threat of a nuclear holocaust – is reflected in the personal extremism of the artists, as though, like diplomats, they had to tread with ever increasing wariness in the knowledge of total disaster – a knowledge which they have obtained by an endless series of underground tests on themselves. No doubt all this is true. But the fact that it is the Americans rather than the Europeans or Russians who have responded to this situation with such artistic alacrity is due, I think, to their peculiar genius for loneliness which creates these conditions even despite the environment.

The Marxists invoke extremism and 'negative' art as evidence of the decline of capitalist society. But the opposite is equally true: because society as a whole is so flourishing, powerful and rich, the artists, in their role of outsiders, feel that they must pay the price of the collective success. It is as though they regarded society's existential failings not just as their responsibility but as their own personal guilt. If their anxiety is unprecedented in its ubiquity and intensity, that is because they are unable to find scapegoats for it outside their own selves. Hence their positive obligation to make the worst of a good thing. The fact that, like most other citizens, they are well fed, well clothed, well housed, well paid, increases their inner sense of trouble. Even to live in a political system that works becomes frustrating: you can vote, help change the party in power, and yet not make a jot of difference to the benevolent anonymity of society itself, which goes on proliferating like a cancer at the expense of the live cells. So even the liberal–humanist position – part of that powerful Jewish influence in American life – seems to be undergoing some crisis of nerves. Each new issue – particularly each promising one – is so swiftly, sophisticatedly and sceptically criticized that there is never even a momentary resting place for optimism. Of course, the destruction is brilliant, witty, stimulating, tart; but it is so only for the sake of brilliance, wit, stimulation, tartness. Attack for the sake of attack is an automatic response, another product perhaps of the isolation and restless drive. So, in a curious way, intellectual energy becomes a means of promoting hopelessness.

Liberal humanism was, I suppose, a hand-down from the thirties, an attempt to carry over into cultural affairs enlightened left-wing principles in a non-political form. As such, it suffered the same fate as Adlai Stevenson (and did so perhaps because of Stevenson's fate): defeat, decline, and then official establishment in a grandiose but essentially unimportant position in the hierarchy of power. Just as Kennedy, compared with Stevenson, represented a political attitude which was at once more stirring, tough-minded, adroit and less tenderly principled, so too in the arts: the attitude is now more ruthless, nihilistic and egocentric than anything foreseen by the liberal tradition. Lionel Trilling may have hit on the difference in the titles of his books; *The Liberal Imagination* gave way to *The Opposing Self*.

But when artists begin to internalize everything – nature and society, art and life, intimacy and response – they have to face a simple but overbearing difficulty: beyond a certain point, the self is also boring. Which is perhaps only another way of saying that the self contains a great deal of destructiveness which it turns as equally against itself as against the outer world. The result is a bored moral nihilism which makes artists of all kinds expend immense intellectual and creative energy in the effort to cut away the ground from under their own feet. Extremism in the arts – the cultivation of breakdown and all the diverse facets of schizophrenia – ends not so much in anarchy as in a kind of internal fascism by which the artist, to relieve his own boredom, becomes both torturer and tortured. This may in no way affect his political enlightenment or general liberal stance. It is simply a question of his attitude to himself and his work: ruthless, destructive, deeply self-involved, wildly self-gratifying. Even the cult of the Absurd, for example, is simply a charming and objective way of rephrasing this internal nihilism: you acknowledge the sureness with which universal darkness buries all, the inevitability of the descent into blank chaos, and then you make a joke about it all. Which is in itself the final nihilism, since it destroys even the force of your under-standing of destruction. Lord Snow picked the wrong example when he ticked off the arts men for not under-standing the Second Law of Thermodynamics. The whole of modern art centres on it: it is concerned, that is, with the principle of psychic entropy, by which the artist's whole world tends continually to run down towards dis-order and disintegration. Thus a work of art, like a law of physics, becomes an attempt to halt the dissolution by a clear, ordered but temporary system of insights. Uncer-tainty has always been a stimulus; now it is also an artistic principle.

In the context of general American *bonhomie*, together-ness and wealthy self-satisfaction, the intense anxiety of the artist is healthy and necessary. But the immediate context in which art is made is that of the creator himself, and maybe a few friends. And there the nihilism is much harder to handle, the isolation harder to accept. Perhaps the continually dissatisfied creative drive towards new forms, new systems, new insights is simply an attempt to find some means of making tolerable those two opposing pressures: the mass pressure of the collective unity of material power, and the lonely pressure of energy turned in and pressing down in utter isolation.